NOT ALL MEMORIES ARE "PRECIOUS"

by

Harold G. Duck

ISBN:

eBook: 979-8-90224-196-6

Paperback: 979-8-90224-197-3

Hardback: 979-8-90224-198-0

Published by:

Authors Publishing House

178 Broadway, 3rd Floor, #1343

New York, NY 10001, USA

Main Line: (855) 624-0155

Email: support@authorspublishinghouse.com

Table of Contents

Not All Memories Are Precious is an unfiltered and deeply personal memoir that captures the complexity of an ordinary man's extraordinary journey through family life, faith, military service, work, and personal trials. The strength of the book lies in its raw honesty and conversational tone, allowing readers to feel as though they are sitting across from the author as he recounts both the tender and painful truths of his past. Its straightforward storytelling style makes it highly accessible. What stands out most, however, is the candor of the author as he does not shy away from exposing his flaws, doubts about religion, and the lessons drawn from hardship, which lends the book a rare authenticity. It is less a polished literary memoir and more a living testament to resilience, faith, and the enduring need to record one's story in full, precious or not.

For anyone who is looking for an uplifting book with rich themes and many life lessons on resilience, strength, and hope, this book is an inspiration and absolutely a must-read. This book is worth reading and a deeply personal look into life.

Dedication

I started this book years ago, but never got around to having it published. Much of the delay was due to the serious illness of my dear wife, Carolyn, who succumbed to her maladies and, after seven months of turmoil, passed away on October 16, 2024. She displayed extraordinary courage during her prolonged suffering and died with the assurance that she displayed and maintained her bravery and spirit until the very end. We were married for forty-four years. Now, with her passing, I finally have the time to pursue my goal of completing this task. I dedicate this book to her memory and her loving support during the entire ordeal.

Acknowledgements

Many thanks to the people who assisted me in this endeavor, especially to my late wife Carolyn Joyce (CJ), and my sisters Dean, who passed away in 2022, and Nina, who spent countless hours reading and re-reading the text, correcting typos, adding notes that I had forgotten and deleting some that were better left unsaid, and my good friend Henry Wood who contributed some inspiring stories and forgotten episodes, and assisted in its publication. I could not have done it without their help. Thanks, too, to the Authors Publishing House and their competent staff who were so very patient with me as we put everything together.

Introduction

There must be hundreds of books out there on every topic and accomplishment you can imagine, about sports figures, movie stars, highly successful businessmen and women, political giants, religious people, etc. You name it, and it is on the shelf at your favorite bookstore. Well, this book is not about any of that; not a famous person; not a superstar; not a super wealthy guru; not a fireball preacher. Nothing. This is the story of a normal, common, ordinary, mediocre person who lived an uneventful life; about his recollections of growing up in the deep South in a very common family; about his ups and downs with religion and churches; his experiences and his thoughts on life. You know, something that most people can identify with. (I know, I ended a sentence with a preposition; a no-no, but, hey, it's my book, so I can do whatever I want). This is a book written in very common language and with no big words. You will not have to look in the dictionary to find the meaning of a word. The idea of writing a book has been on my mind for many of my eighty-two years, and I never took the time or made the effort to carry through with it. I think it is time to do it. I wrote it because I could not find a story about an ordinary person with no big or glamorous outcome. It really does not offer any advice about any subject, but it is my hope that you can identify with some of its content and can pick up a good idea along the way. The Title of this Book came from a comment of my aged Dad, when he was listening to the Gospel Song "Precious Memories," said, "You know, not all memories are precious' and he was exactly right. This Book captures those memories, which are sometimes 'precious' and oft times are not. So sit back, relax, and enjoy it.

About The Author

Harold Gray Duck started writing at an early age. In his ninth-grade literature class he would not only write poetry as a class assignment, but he also wrote additional poems for his classmates who were terrified at the thought of writing anything past their own name. He wrote short stories throughout his high school and college days and wrote one or more feature articles for the college paper. He was the sportswriter for the college baseball and basketball teams, and wrote a syndicated column published in fourteen newspapers. His paper on Effective Written Communication is filed in the Fort Belvoir, Virginia library. He writings today include over 200 Sunday School lessons. His personal and touching story about the untimely and tragic death of Wally, the little Black Poodle who was so much loved by his family, is a must for any animal lover who has suffered the grief of a family pet. Duck's simple and personal style has a way of bringing to life the joys of loving and caring for a pet, and will help any pet owner go through the pain of a loss. This inexpensive short story is an excellent gift for anyone who has experienced this tragedy.

Chapter One
The Beginning
1943

As the old saying goes, "I was born at a very early age" to Davis Carl and Cora Lou Duck. Davis Duck was a tall, slim, rugged, primitive, strong, outdoor, part Indian (or Native American, to be politically correct) man, who trapped animals in the Tensaw River Delta swamps for a living until he was twenty-nine years old, when the lady who was to become my mom trapped and tamed him (somewhat). So Dad left the river swamps to begin a family life on thirty acres of land in Baldwin County, Alabama, that he purchased from Mr. Ewing, who lived in Yonkers, New York. He then bought a small four-room shack from his brother and moved it onto his land, which he called a farm. The house consisted of two bedrooms, a living room, and a kitchen. It had no electricity and no heat. Dad was actually a sharecropper for his brother, but the land he lived on was not ready for farming; he had to clear it first by cutting the trees and removing the stumps. He did this by digging a deep hole around the stumps and then using a long-handled drill to bore a hole near the base. Then he would place a stick of dynamite in the hole, light a fuse, and blow the stump out of the ground. I have been told that he would sometimes take me with him when I was as young as two years old on these excursions, but thank goodness I never got blown up. But I do remember going with him later1

I can recall running like crazy to get away from the explosion, ad them being mesmerized by a stump flying through the air fifty feet above the ground.

This was my place of birth, in that little shack delivered by a country doctor who made house calls. I was there, but I don't remember much about it, if anything at all. I have been told things about it that I have no reason to doubt, so I have accepted them as fact. I was born at 4:15 a.m. (I was not very considerate of my mother) on a cold and rainy April 1, 1943. I have lived with the name Duck and an April Fool's boy all my life. I used to take offense at all the jokes, but I got tired of being beaten up in the third grade. Since then, I have become pretty insensitive to duck jokes, although I still hear them regularly.

I also recall that the little shack had a front porch, and my parents had hung a swing from the rafter at the edge of the porch. It had a seat in it, and they would tie me in there, where I was happy and entertained for hours at a time. Now I suspect that they used that swing to get me out of their hair and out of the house. But, hey, I was happy and so were they. I also had a favorite hiding place in the house, and that was underneath the bed – mother and dad's bed. I don't think I had a bed. I don't really recall where I, or my younger brother, slept, but I think it was on a pallet on the living room floor. My two older sisters shared the other bed room. Anyway, the bedspread hung nearly to the floor and created a private cave as it were, and I used to enjoy lying on my back and playing with the dust in the bed-springs.

Chapter Two
The Old Place
1944

At that little shack I told you about, we had a water well in the back yard; one with a spool and a crank, a water bucket, and a rope. The well housing was about twelve inches wide, twelve inches deep, and about six feet tall. Now, as you read this, you need to remember that this was back in the 1940's, so if you are young, you will have to use your imagination. I still remember the sound of that water bucket splashing when it hit the water at the bottom of the well. The bucket was about six inches in diameter and about thirty inches long. It was tied to a rope, which was probably thirty or forty feet long. The well was not very deep, but it did produce clear, cool, good-tasting water. We would draw water from the well and pour it into the water bucket on the back porch, where a common dipper was used by everyone who wanted a drink of water. Periodically, the well would go dry, and we would take the water bucket to a nearby spring and fill it there, along with debris and insects and tadpoles and whatever else may have been lurking in the waters. Then we would empty the water bucket into the drinking pail on the water shelf on the back porch, and everyone would enjoy a drink. I shudder to think what diseases we would contract by doing that in today's world.

I was the third child and the second son. In 1941, Mother gave birth to her third child, her first son, and my Dad was ecstatic. He had wanted a son so badly, but had gotten two girls so far, and he couldn't wait to pass out cigars to celebrate the birth of his son. But sadly, Wayne Davis died when he was only nine days old, due to a bacteria in the mother's milk. Dad almost went crazy and actually thought of taking his own life, but because of his faith in God and his devotion to his family, he managed to get through it all. However, to his dying day he would still talk about his first-born son and the tragedy he suffered. I soon realized that I may be the first surviving son, but I would never take the place of 'Son #1'.

Chapter Three
The New House
1947

Dad added another ten acres to his 'farm,' and in 1946, he built a new house for his family, almost single-handedly and without the benefit of electricity or power tools. It was a fine house with a large living room, a formal dining room, a kitchen, three bedrooms, a front porch across the entire width of the house, and a nice-sized back porch. We moved to it in 1947 when I was four. My job during the move was to stand in the back of Uncle Fred's pickup truck and prevent the furniture from falling over. We actually moved in before the back bedrooms were finished, so we had a one-bed in the dining room and another in the living room, where my younger sister was delivered three years later by the same county doctor who had brought my two other sisters, my brother, and me into the world. In fact, my mother delivered twins, but she came dangerously close to dying as she gave birth, and the doctor told my dad he had to make a choice between the twin girls and his wife. Dad told him, "Save my wife," so the doctor laid the twins aside when they were born. After he had stabilized my mom, he turned to the twins and was able to save one of them. The other had already died, so we had a birth and a death at the same time.

Our new house also had a hand-pump, so now we did not have to draw water from the well. We did, however, have to pump water for the water bucket, and in a big tub for our horse, and for the wash-pot when mother washed clothes in the back yard, and later on, for her wringer washing machine when she got her new Maytag. This house had a dirt yard, which we had to keep clean of debris, grass, and weeds. We made yard-brooms from the sage grass that grew wild in the fields. Dwight and I also spent many an hour playing cars and trucks in the dirt underneath the front porch. A couple of things that I still remember about the new house were going to sleep on the living room floor every Saturday night, listening to the Grand Ole Opry on the radio while Mother was ironing our Sunday clothes. And every night, Daddy would pick me up and put me in bed without ever waking me. I also remember waking up on cold winter mornings and hearing a rip-roaring fire in the living room fireplace. That was the only heat in the house, and I would stand as close to that fire as I could to get dressed. I would burn up on one side while freezing on the other. And when my backside was as hot as I could stand it, my brother would walk by and pull my trousers against my legs.

Another memory of my younger days were haircuts. Mother was our barber, and I hated her haircuts with a passion. She used the old-fashioned manual hand-operated clippers, and they always got tangled up in my hair. Then she would yank them, and I would lose a clump of hair with a loud scream. I recall telling her that when I was grown, I was never going to get another haircut. Thankfully, in my pre-teen years, Daddy started taking us to the barber shop in town, and Mr. Si Thompson was a lot less painful than was my dear old mom. And that was where I first got introduced to 'barber-shop talk' while my Dad would grimace, and ever once in a while, he would remind some old country yokel to watch his language because a young boy was present.

Our old house became the storage place for our crops – mostly cotton and corn. I can still recall playing in the corn crib and watching corn snakes crawling on the rafters above our heads. Speaking of snakes, we grew up with them. We learned how to identify and respect the poisonous ones, and ignore or play with the others. At one time, I caught a small green snake and made a pet of him. I would scare cousins and neighbors out of their minds with him. One day, Dwight took him to school, which almost got him expelled. But lo, Mr. Green Snake grew up and left home. I did get bitten three times, one of which was by a pygmy rattler, which put me flat on my back for about six weeks. It happened late one afternoon when I was walking home along the narrow trail from the old house where mother had been milking the cow. I saw him along the edge of the woods just as I took a step close to his head, but it was too late, and he popped me. My leg immediately became numb, and my mother picked me up and carried me to Uncle Fred's house, and my dad borrowed his truck to drive me to the doctor. Dr. McLeod treated me on his front porch. He used a suction cup to draw out the poison, then covered the bite with a dark grease, and took me home. During that six-week recovery period, I recall neighbors bringing me comic books and ice cream. I said 'You know what – this snake bite was not all that bad.' The other two were not poisonous and required no trip to the doctor. One happened while Dad, Dwight, and I were walking home along a dirt road after a day of fishing. He was a short brown snake, and I asked Dad, 'Will he bite?' and Dad said, 'No, he won't bite you, meaning he was not poisonous, but I took him literally and stuck my foot right to his nose, and he popped me. Then Dad said, 'Of course, if you do that, he will bite you; I meant he was not poisonous.' That was the end of it. We continued walking home. I never went to a doctor. I really do not recall the third bite, but it was not harmful either.

Dwight and I spent a lot of time at the old house that stored our crops, but was also a home for the farm animals. One day we were playing around in the hog pen when Dwight decided to pick up a new-born shoat, who squealed like crazy, and made his big mama sow come running to his rescue. I thought we had met our end, but Dwight dropped that little pig and somehow managed to jump over the four-foot fence and escape. We never again wanted to hold a new little pig in our arms. In addition to the hogs, we had a few other farm animals; a couple of cows, a mule who died of old age, an old plow mare who got stuck in a bog down by the creek, developed pneumonia, and died, and a Calico pony that dad bought for us boys to ride. But that pony did not last long because he was mean and would try to run over us when we stepped into his pasture. The old house also offered a temptation that we could not resist. It still had all the windows intact, and we decided it would be fun to take a pole and break every one of them. The trouble was, we were unaware of the time, and just as we finished the last one, Mr. Duck walked up behind us. He did not give us the whipping we deserved, but after the tongue-lashing we endured, I kind of wish he had.

Chapter Four
My Four-Legged Friends
1948

I remember my best companion when I was very young was 'Ole Rattler'. Ole Rattler was a black and tan hound that Daddy got from Mr. Buck Harvill. Actually, he got two hounds, a brother and a sister. The Sister was Cindy, and she belonged to my brother Dwight. I think part of the reason he got those hounds was because Mother told him, "We ain't having no dogs around here". But he told her every boy needed a dog, so two it was. Now, me and 'Ole Rattler' were good buddies. We would ramble the woods together, and I still remember sitting in the front porch swing and sharing a bologna sandwich. I would take a bite and then give my four-legged buddy a bite. But eventually, both of the hounds died, and we got a little dog named Rusty. He was a good dog, too, and he would eat anything that we ate, including tomato sandwiches. But one day, when the Preacher's wife walked up with her baby in her arms, Rusty dashed out from under the front porch and nipped her on the leg. Well, Daddy couldn't have any of that, so he gave Rusty to his friend, Dwight, and I grieved. But lo and behold, almost a year later, while we were playing in the back yard on Thanksgiving afternoon, Rusty came running up. Man, were we glad; we had a happy reunion, and much to our delight, Daddy said if Rusty wanted to live with us that badly, he could stay. So he did until he died of old age.

We had a lot of dogs, but with your indulgence, I will tell you of only a couple more. Bobo was an English Bulldog, white with one black spot around his right eye. We had a lot of fun with Bobo as well, and spent hours on end in the woods hunting snakes. Bobo did not like snakes, and he would search them out, and then chew them up and down their spine, and then shake them so vigorously that sometimes their heads would pop off. Trouble was, Bobo hated cats as much as he hated snakes, and he started going around the neighborhood looking for cats, which he would promptly kill. One day, Bobo came limping home, barely able to walk. Someone had shot him with a shotgun, and he forced himself to come home and tell us goodbye. We gave him some warm milk, but he would not drink it. We gave him a hot dog, but he would not eat it. He licked our hands and then turned and walked away into the woods. We never saw Bobo again, although we looked for him. Bless his heart! And bless ours, too. Man, did we ever cry for Bobo. The last one I will tell you about was one of my favorites. His name was Buster. As I walked by the bulletin board at the office one day, I noticed a note from a lady that said she was giving her dog to someone who would offer him a good home. I went to see her and followed her home to get him. His name was Buster, and he was an AKC-registered Sheltie. He was a beautiful dog. When I got home with him, I walked him around the perimeter of our land, and since that day, Buster has been a protector of our place. He loved to play ball and actually taught our other dog, Sandy, to fetch and retrieve. Buster died of cancer when he was ten years old. I still think of him from time to time, even to this day. Okay, enough about dogs. Let's get back to our humble dwelling.

Chapter Five
Sisters Three
1950

I have talked a lot about my brother, Dwight, because Dwight and I did a lot together. But I also had three sisters –the two who were older and one younger. My oldest Sister, Mary Lunell (called Nell), was six years older than I was, and we never spent a lot of time together. I do remember that we both enjoyed reading and writing, and sometimes we would talk about a book or article we had read. We also liked to tell jokes and would try to outdo each other with new ones. Nell married a man straight out of the Navy when she was seventeen. Bob was an interesting character, and he used his friendship with Dwight and me in order to get in the good graces of our older sister. He spent time with us playing ball or intentionally disturbing a wasp nest and running like crazy to keep from getting stung. We usually crouched down low in the cotton patch and watched them fly above our heads. Bob was also a pretty good musician and could play the piano and the guitar. In fact, he was playing at the Breesy Pines, a local honky-tonk when Nell met him. He was also a decent singer. Later, Nell led Bob to Jesus Christ, and eventually Bob became Dr. Robert Mitchell Jaye, Sr., a Baptist Minister. He is the one who persuaded me to attend Carey College later on. But being a preacher meant that he and Nell moved a lot, and consequently, that meant that she and I saw less of each other. However, Nell was wise, and she frequently offered me a bit of advice concerning my life and lifestyle. I think she minored in French, and I took French in high school, so I was able to speak two or three sentences with her – like "What time is it?' Close the door, please. "Hello, Madame." and "Do you speak French?" That was about the extent of my French vocabulary. I was told that she had written two novels, one in French and another in English. When Bob enrolled at William Carey College in Hattiesburg, Mississippi, Nell took a job and worked to put her husband through college. Nell always wanted to go to college herself, but they could not afford it. But after her sons were grown and gone, she fulfilled her dream by enrolling at the University of Alabama and graduating in 1980. Nell contracted cancer and died in 1993 at the age of fifty-five. After her death, I asked Bob for her novels, but he could not find them. So I never got to read her books. Nell had two sons, Robert Mitchell Jr. and Davis Monroe.

Erma Dean (Dean) was four years older than I, and she, too, never had a real close relationship with me. But Dean was the sister I could identify with most. She had a mind of her own that did not necessarily align with the teachings of her parents. (Neither did mine). Dean was ambitious and venturous. She attended Carey College for a semester, but that was not her cup of tea, so she dropped out and got a job. She owned a couple of businesses and lived in various places in Alabama, Mississippi, Georgia, and Florida. She married a man named Lavonne O'Gwynn and had two sons by him – Martin and Russell. After twenty-seven years of marriage, she and Lavonne divorced, and she later married a man named Jerry Hudson. He and Dean were married over thirty years, lived in Shalimar, Florida, and then moved to Wetumpka, Alabama. Dean contracted Hopkins disease, spent her last two years bedridden, and died in February 2022. One year later, Jerry decided he could not live without her, and took his own life in

February 2023.

Nina Miriam was, and is, my younger sister. Dwight and I used to give Nina a hard time. We were always playing some kind of mean trick on her. I was told that we would climb a young pine sapling to the top, ride it down to the ground, and then tie Nina to it and turn it loose so we could watch her swing back and forth. I don't know if that is true, but that is one of her tales. I do know we would sneak into her room, put a chair in front of the window, dress it in bluejeans, a shirt, put a football and a hat for a head, and then laugh when she got ready for bed and screamed at its silhouette. I guess I felt closer to Nina than I did to my older sisters, because she lived in our house after the other girls had moved out. I also recall giving her a quarter to scare herself whenever I would bring a date to our house. Nina was, and has been, my biggest supporter. Through all my hard times, stupid decisions, and wayward lifestyle, Nina was always in my corner. She never criticized me or tried to get me to change. She always understood me in a way no-one else did, including my own Mother. As best I can remember, she spent a semester at Carey too, as Dean had done. Nina worked for years at Quincy Compressor and held an important mid-level management job there. She also lived in Florida for a few years, and married a man named Ken Hofman while she was there. And like Dean and me, Nina has her own sideline business after retirement. She and Ken make furniture, and Nina creates some pretty jewelry. Even though she is the youngest in the family, she and Ken have set the record in marriage years, by celebrating over fifty-five years together. Nina has two daughters, Rhonda and Heather.

Now, a final note on Dwight. Dwight and I enjoyed growing up together in the woods. We spent many days hunting for snakes with Bobo, and we usually had no trouble finding plenty of them. Then, some days, we would dig caves into the sides of the deep gully behind our house. Only the good Lord took care of his two little children and kept us from being buried underneath a pile of dirt or killed by a rattlesnake or deadly moccasin. Actually, one of our friends in Bay Minette was buried alive when the roof of his cave fell in on him. And like all brothers, some days we fought. I was a bit stronger, but Dwight was faster. I recall hitting him in the mouth one day and then running like crazy when he picked up a long file and attempted to attack me with it. He caught up with me in the front yard and let the file fly, hitting me in the back. Luckily, it was the blunt end, so I ended up with a minor scratch rather than a file sticking out of my back. Dwight worked in the newspaper industry his entire adult life, starting out with the Baldwin Times in Bay Minette, where he worked for Mr. Jimmy Faulkner. After he graduated from High School, he moved to Hattiesburg to be with me and worked at the Hattiesburg American. He later worked in Houston and finished his career at the Mobile Register. He married a woman named Faye Cochran from Hattiesburg in 1964. Shortly after they got married, Dwight enlisted in the Air Force, and they lived in Warner Robbins, Georgia, for three years and three months. He was deployed to DaNang, Vietnam, for his last nine months. After his discharge, they first rented a house in Hattiesburg, until they moved to Mobile. They spent the majority of their married life in and around Mobile. He was exposed to Agent Orange in Vietnam, and later suffered from front lobal dimensia which took his life in 2007 at age sixty-two.

Dwight was a good Christian man and a much better brother than I deserved. I still miss him. He and Faye did not have any children.

So now you know the family. I have three sisters, two brothers, and two parents who are now in heaven, and only one sister is still alive. Oh, one more thing about Nina. She was always upset with me because I had three sisters and she only had two. Go figure!

Chapter Six
Cousins and the Farm
1952

We had a varied childhood, with good times and bad. We had tons of cousins, so we got together on a regular basis, and had family reunions at Grandmother's house every year. We also entertained ourselves by having wars with clogs of dirt, bows and arrows, B-B guns, and anything else we could use as a weapon. We were poor and learned to work hard for a living. You have heard people say, "We were poor, but we didn't know it. Well, we were poor, and I knew it very well. I wore three-dollar Dickie bluejeans to school while my friends wore ten-dollar Levi's, and I wore homemade shirts that my mother sewed from feed sacks. I hated those shirts and only later in life learned to appreciate the sacrifice that my parents made for us. I recall that Dad bought a horse, a wagon, and three or four implements from Mrs. Ruple for $200, which was a whopping amount of money in 1948, and which resulted in one of the biggest fusses I witnessed between Mother and Daddy. But the deal was done, and the horse and wagon stayed. Of course, we boys were thrilled, and we rode many a mile in that wagon. Dad incorporated the additional ten acres he purchased, but of the forty, he only cleared and farmed about nine or ten. We became farmhands as soon as we were able to work. I remember coming home from school in the first grade and changing from my school clothes to my work clothes and eating a peanut butter and jelly sandwich on the way to the cotton field where we picked until it was too dark to see that stuff. I never saw any money from all that cotton picking, but my two sisters did get a piano out of it. I did not enjoy picking cotton, although I never hated pulling corn. One day, when Dad was plowing the rows for corn, and Dwight and I were dropping the corn seeds in them and covering them with dirt, Dwight decided to take a shortcut by dropping all his seeds in at once at the beginning of the row. Dad did not know this until the corn sprouted, and needless to say, he was not too happy about it. After he had 'explained' it to him, Dwight understood that he should never do that again. Enough said!

When I was a bit older, I decided to pick cotton for some of the local farmers and got paid a whopping $.03 per pound. One day, I picked up eight whole pounds and got tipped a penny by being paid a quarter. That job did not last too long. I recall hearing that Charlie Pride once said, "I don't know what I am going to do when I grow up, but I know that I ain't gonna pick cotton. Well, Charlie Pride and I had that in common. As was the case with Charlie Pride, I think that those cotton fields helped motivate me to pursue a higher and easier style of living. Another short job was at the potato shed in Loxley. Man, that was hard work from dawn to dark, and then we slept on burlap sacks on the wooden floor. My job was to push an old, antiquated, oversized, two-wheel dolly loaded with corn from the loading dock to the train car and then to spray it down with crushed ice. I quit after two days of that back-breaking job. One year, the Government paid Dad not to plant cotton, and that was one of my favorite years. Several years later, Dad decided to quit farming and plant the entire area in pine trees. I never realized any reward from the pine trees either, but I did like not farming, and was glad our farming days were over.

Chapter Seven
Jesus Loves Me
1952

We need to back up a few years here, but it fits better here than in the chronological order of things. In March 1952, we had a revival led by an evangelist named Peter Ruckman, and one night he preached a sermon that I thought was meant only for me. He was a chalk artist, and he would draw a picture as he preached. That particular night, I was really convicted of my sins and realized I needed Jesus Christ as a Savior. You see, sometimes, before I had committed the sins of lying and stealing. We had a neighbor about our age, and one day, when we were over at his house playing, I noticed he had a wristwatch; not a real watch, mind you, but a play one that did not keep time. Nevertheless, I was fascinated with that watch, so when no one was looking, I stole it. Back at our house the next day, I said to my brother Dwight, "Let's go out in the pasture and see if we can find anything, so we did, and lo and behold, I found a watch – the one I had lifted a day prior. I was elated! I had a watch of my own and no one was the wiser – except dear ole mom, that is. She had a way of knowing everything, and she did not buy the story of its miraculous appearance in the cow pasture. So she 'persuaded' me to return the watch to its original owner and apologize. That was not enjoyable!

And then I lied. My little sister Nina had a bicycle that was her pride and joy. One day, I decided it would be fun to turn the bike upside down and stand on its handlebars. I have no idea why I thought that, but that is exactly what I did, and when I did it, the handlebars broke right off. Well, I knew I could not explain that to my mother, and the only logical explanation that I could think of was that our dog jumped over Nina's bicycle, hit the handlebars, and knocked them right off. For some unknown reason, mother did not buy that story any more than she believed the tale about the watch in the pasture. I don't know what it was about that woman!

Anyway, during Rev. Peter's sermon, those two sins popped up in my mind, and I was convicted big time. To this day, I remember what he preached about and the picture he drew as he preached. I knew I had sinned and that I was headed straight for hell. But I didn't do anything and did not say anything to anyone. But during the night, my mother heard me crying and came to check on me. I remember saying to her, "I don't want to go to hell; I don't want to go to hell. She told me that I did not have to go to hell; that Jesus provided a way out, and explained to me how to get saved. I tell you what – the next night at the revival service, I don't remember a thing about the sermon, but I could not wait until it ended. At the first note of "Just As I Am," I was down that aisle to the front, telling the preacher I wanted to get saved. That was just a week short of my ninth birthday. Now I tell people I was saved under the preaching of Peter and Paul. I am sorry to say that my commitment to Jesus has not always been as strong as it was that night. But I sure am glad he did not decide to throw me away. And I sure am glad that he had a tender place in his heart for little children. I have often wondered since I became an adult if I really knew what I was doing that night, and if I really was saved. Then I think of the time that Jesus said, 'Unless you become like one of these little children, you will not see the

Kingdom of God.' Then it makes sense. You see, little children are trusting and their minds are moldable. They don't know all the stuff that can cause them to question everything and doubt their salvation. I talk a little more about this in the next chapter.

Chapter Eight
Fist-Ta-Cuffs
1954

I was not a good fighter. I was always the 97-pound weakling growing up. There was one kid in elementary school who was a bully and who always picked fights with me because I was an easy target. This gave me an inferiority complex, which haunted me all through grammar school. I was always the last one chosen to be on the ball team. One day, when I was in the fifth grade, I was challenged to a fist fight and accepted the challenge. I don't have any idea what brought it on. I also have no idea why I accepted the challenge, but for some unknown reason, I did. It was prearranged for a time and place on the school grounds after classes, and a circle of students surrounded us as we prepared to get it on. Then all the kids started rooting for my opponent, and that really devastated me. I started crying and ran away. There was no fight that day, but I lost all the same. I have wished since then that my Dad or an uncle had taught me how to fight and defend myself. It probably would have resulted in a bit more self-respect plus a few black eyes or bloody noses, but at least I would not have been the push-over I was. When thinking of my fighting, I am reminded of the guy who said, 'I hit him in the face with my nose so many times that blood was everywhere.

Chapter Nine
First Cars
1955

When I was twelve, in 1955, the horse and wagon was abandoned or sold or something, and Dad bought a car – a 1947 Chevrolet – from Mr. Fuqua in Stapleton for $150.00, and I learned how to drive. In 1958, Dad bought a 1956 Chevrolet from Carlton Boutwell, and I flipped it end over end not too long after that. Thank the Good Lord I came away without even a scratch. When I was a Senior in High School, I bought my first car, a 1951 Ford, for $175.00 with the help of my Mother. This time it was Dad's turn to hit the ceiling. I have never understood why it upset him so, but he really got mad. I think it must have been because Mother and I did it without his knowledge or without asking for his permission. After that, Dad made me a deal – I could claim the family car, the 1956 Chevy, as mine, and he would trade my 1951 Ford for a pickup. I didn't have a vote in the matter, and I lost my car. Then, in 1962, Dad bought a Ford Falcon from the dealership in Atmore, and I rolled it too. Dwight was with me, and again, we were not injured. Dad was pretty understanding about the first one; not so much the second time. But a year later, when I was a Sophomore in College, my Brother-in-Law, Bob Jaye, bought a 1951 Chevy and gave it to me.

I have always liked cars. Years ago, I decided to list all the cars I had owned, and I quit counting when I got to 42. I have probably had 42 more since then. My friend, Don Carter, once told me, "You change cars as often as I change socks, which was almost true. I sure wish I still had the 1950 and 1960 models I used to own. I have had a 1951 Ford, a 1953 Ford, a 1957 Ford, two 1966 Ford Mustangs, a 1951 Chevrolet, a 1955 Chevy, two 1956 Chevys, a 1959 Chevy, a 1965 Chevy, a 1956 Pontiac, two 1964 Ramblers, and maybe a couple I have forgotten. I bought the '55 Chevy for $500 with the engine and the transmission in the back seat. After thinking about it for a day or so, I decided that was more than I wanted to tackle, and I sold it for $500. Why in the world didn't I keep those toys? Boy, hind-sight is wonderful, ain't it? And that doesn't even count the pickups. I had one 1965 Chevy, which was a long wheelbase step-side. And one of my favorites was a 1974 Chevrolet Cheyenne with a 454 cubic inch engine. Man, would that thing run! I did not lose many races. But it would not pass up a service station. It was a gas-guzzler. I also bought a 1964 Chevy Step-side short wheel base in 2007, which I restored. It was a beauty and turned a lot of heads every time I drove it. But as old trucks go (as well as old men), there was something that always needed fixing on it, so I finally sold it.

Chapter Ten
Religion
1956

My parents were very religious. I have always said that they were much more religious than they were Christian. They believed in God and were dedicated to the church. In fact, I tell people that I started going to church nine months before I was born. I don't think that was literally true, because in the 1940's it was the practice of pregnant women to seclude themselves when they started showing signs of pregnancy. So it was more likely I went to church for the first three months and then took a six-month leave of absence until I was born and old enough to go again. Oh My Goodness! Did I use the word 'pregnant'? That was not said aloud back then. Instead, some lady would whisper to a friend, 'You know she is 'pg', don't you?' But after that time had elapsed, I was there every Sunday and Wednesday. But as religious as my Mother and Daddy were, they did not always act like Christians. They were God-loving people for sure; they just did not always act like it at home. I recall many fusses between them, sometimes involving the church. Mother was a seamstress, and the upper right-hand drawer on her Singer sewing machine was known as the 'Tithe Drawer'. When Dad got paid, he would stick 10% of his pay in the tithe drawer. At times, Mother would 'borrow' from the cash in the tithe drawer, and that would set him off into a rage. I feel sure that she always paid it back, but that did not stop my Pop from blowing his stack. Dad had a hair-trigger temper, and Mother knew exactly how7to push his buttons. She would disagree with almost everything he said; she would criticize him, ridicule him, respond sarcastically, and humiliate him in public. This would set Dad into a rage. I really think these tirades had a lasting effect on me that continues to influence my decisions even to this day. If there is one thing that I detest, it is to be ridiculed – especially in public. Speaking of tithing, my Mother once told me something that no one should tell a fifteen-year-old boy. I had two friends – O'Neal and Claude, Jr. O'Neal's family owned a new Buick, and Claude's family owned a new Oldsmobile. This was in 1956. Man, those were beautiful automobiles! One day, as I was lamenting over our old 1947 Chevy, my Mother told me, "But honey, those people do not tithe. If we did not tithe, we could afford a car like that. For years after that, I would not even think about giving a tithe to a church. But I did have brand new beautiful cars.

Chapter Eleven
Primitive Vs Refined
1956

As I said earlier, my dad was a very primitive, rugged man of Indian descent who preferred living outdoors. He was satisfied with absolutely nothing above a shack or camp and wild animals for food. He would have fit right in with the Mountain Men currently on television. He had no desire for the finer things of life, nor was he interested in acquiring any material possessions. He took great pride in teaching his two sons how to hunt and fish. And he taught us the correct way to paddle a boat, from the right side only. He would tell us, "If you have to paddle from both sides, then just put the paddle down when another boat passes. I recall one fishing trip when Dad was paddling our boat, and we saw a boat with a small outboard motor ahead. Well, that little boat kept getting larger and larger, and eventually Dad, with his paddle, passed that boat with the motor. He basically told my mom, "Hey, you raise the girls; I will handle the boys. He loved us, although he seldom told us, and he loved spending time with us. And he could be very strict and harsh when he caught us doing wrong. On the other side, he was extremely hard-working and honest. I recall him walking about six miles to town to pay a merchant a penny that he owed him from an earlier purchase.

Mother was just the opposite. Her family was not rich, but they were comfortable, and she was raised to appreciate the finer things in life. Sadly, she never got many things she desired with my Dad. Mother was a hard worker and an excellent seamstress. Not only did she sew clothes for friends and neighbors, but she also made things like cheerleader uniforms, wedding dresses, draperies, and such. I loved it when she made those cheerleader uniforms because the house would be full of good-looking girls in short skirts. She became renowned and sought after as a seamstress, and was hired by Strong's Department Store as their alteration specialist, and later held the same position at the Service Dry Cleaners for Mrs. Mae Byars. She would spend her money on things for the house, like paint for the walls, linoleum for the floors, curtains for the windows, etc. All of this made Dad mad. He did not like the fact that his wife "had to work" for them to make a living. He fussed about everything she bought for the house as unnecessary and a waste of money. Mother was a loving person who cared deeply for her children. She would always put her children before her wants. I remember we only had one set of dishes that did not match (we didn't have China), and one plate was cracked. Mother always ate from the cracked plate. And she said she always preferred the chicken back or neck to the legs or breast. That's the kind of person she was. She was profoundly religious and read her Bible daily, prayed a lot – much of it for me. Mother was also stern, and she never backed away from discipline. She probably gave me more whippings than did my dad, even though he had told her to leave the boys to him. I guess she learned that from her Dad. He was a railroad worker with the L&N rail line for most of his life. His lifestyle was structured, time-oriented, disciplined, and he did not want anything to change that. Grandmother had to have dinner (dinner was the mid-day meal back then, not the evening meal) on the table at 11:30 every day when he took his lunch break.

Chapter Twelve
The Bicycle
1957

My goodness. I jumped way ahead. Let's go back to the farm where I was a kid. Besides the snake bites, I also suffered a broken arm. Remember the unfinished house I mentioned earlier. Well, the floor joists were in place, but the floor had not yet been installed. Dad gave us strict orders not to go into those rooms, so quite naturally, they held a curiosity that lured me right in. One day, as I was crawling across the joists, I lost my balance and fell to the ground below, breaking my left arm. Dad was not very impressed with my sense of curiosity or bravery, nor with the extra cost of a doctor's visit. I wore a cast for six weeks, but before my arm healed, I hopped on my bicycle, fell, and broke it again. We did not have a store-bought bike, but being the industrious brothers we were, we scraped enough parts from the garbage dump to make us a homemade version. In fact, our Christmases were quite simple, as Dolly Parton sang "Hard Candy Christmas'. I remember stockings with candy, nuts, fruits, and maybe a little toy. One Christmas, I wished very hard for a cap pistol, and I got up around 4:00 a.m. to see if Santa brought it. Sure enough, there it was, and I was loading it so I could wake up the whole family. Trouble is, when I went tiptoeing through the house, I woke up Mother, who woke up Daddy, and said, "I heard a rat in the house." But Daddy said, "That wasn't a rat – It was Harold," and he appeared with an order to 'Go back to bed' just before I fired my first shot. I waited two more hours for my shooting spree.

Speaking of bicycles, our first new bike came one Christmas when I was about ten years old. That was when I found out the true identity of Santa Claus. Dad bought a bicycle for Dwight and me to share. Were we ever excited when we found it underneath the Christmas tree! All our friends had bicycles, and we did not. However, we noticed that there was mud on the tires and questioned Dad about it. He explained to us that he had hidden the bicycle at our neighbor's house and had retrieved it during the dark on a rainy night, so he had to push it home in the mud. Well, the revelation of 'Daddy-Santa did not lessen our excitement, and we rode that bike all day long.

Chapter Thirteen
Early Church
1957

My earlier joke about going to church nine months before I was born was no joke at all. The church was a very important part of the life of my parents. Dad's father was the Rev. A. D. Duck, a circuit-riding Methodist preacher who traveled throughout Baldwin and Escambia counties in Alabama and sometimes Jackson County in Mississippi and Escambia County, Florida. He was pretty well-known as a loving, kind, and compassionate man who wanted to serve the Lord by serving others. He was one of the organizers and first preachers at a little country church in the Crossroads community known as the Union Church due to the unity of its combined membership of Baptists and Methodists who shared the Church. The Baptists would meet on one Sunday and the Methodists the next Sunday. Grandpa also worked as a logger and road builder. So my dad grew up going to church with his dad. My mother's parents were not as involved, but the church was an important part of their lives. I remember as a little kid, I would stretch out on the third pew on the right side of the auditorium (everyone had their own place to sit, you know, and everyone knew that that was 'our pew'. By the way, we did not encroach on anyone's else's territory either). Anyway, I would stretch out every Sunday night and let the congregation sing me to sleep. And that was some of the best sleep I ever had. I had not learn to snore back then, so I didn't disturb anyone. I also remember my Grandmother's voice as she belted out the words of every hymn in an off-pitch, shrill. And as every young boy did, I sometimes acted in a manner unbecoming to a church-going lad. My uncle Horace had one of those Chevrolet panel-wagon vans with no windows that he used to transport workers to and from their jobs. But at church, it was known as the 'whipping van' used to point out the error of the ways of young lads. I had my time in that van, screaming when I left the church sanctuary and sniffling when I returned. But for the most part, I was a 'good little boy' in church. I rarely missed a Sunday School class; I read the Bible; I answered the questions asked by the teacher, and I enjoyed learning. In fact, I was so good that people sometimes told me that I should be a preacher when I grew up. Trouble is, God never told me that. When I was seven or eight, we had a Pastor named Paul Rowden, who later became a missionary to Israel and died of cancer when he was in his late twenties or early thirties. I really like Bro. Rowden and he liked me too. One day, he let me sit on his lap and steer his 1949 Ford. Man, did I feel grown up and important that day! That was back in 1950. I was seven years old at the time. I recall asking him about my encouragement to become a preacher, and he told me, 'Harold, if you can be happy doing anything else in life, then God is not calling you to preach. Well, God didn't, and I didn't.

Chapter Fourteen
Unchristian Christians
1959

I guess as a young Christian, I expected Christians to live like Christians. Sadly, that is not the case. I saw too many un-Christian episodes in people who professed to be Christians, and that has really confused and impacted me throughout my life. It started in my own home. As religious as my parents were, they did not exemplify the love of Christ that is taught in the Bible. They argued and yelled at each other a lot and would go days without speaking to each other. I almost got a whipping when I was fifteen years old by suggesting to them during one of the fusses, "Why don't y'all get a divorce so at least one of you can be happy?" They quit fussing long enough to turn on me for uttering the "D-word" in their house. Anyway, I grew up sort of confused about what this Christianity stuff was supposed to mean, except for an eternal home in heaven. And, as I am sure is the case with some others who were saved at a very young age, I have wondered 'Was it really real? Did I understand what it all meant? Did I know what was going on? Or was it all an emotional event that never got into my heart'? I remember that on the evening, I got so convicted that three of my friends walked down the aisle to accept Christ as their Savior. Was I just wanting to imitate them? Another thing that caused me to doubt it was the sinful lifestyle I lived for about ten years. Sure, as an adult, I believe that Jesus Christ is the Son of God; that He is the Messiah; and that He died on a cross as the ultimate sacrifice for my sins. Should I now make a public profession of my sincere belief and be baptized again, just in case that occurrence at the age of nine was not real? Then I recall the words of Jesus as He was talking to his disciples when He said, 'Except you become as one of these little children, you will not see the kingdom of God.' And that has always given me the assurance that it was real. You see, little children are accepting, trusting, and believing. And I guess that is good enough for me.

Chapter Fifteen
Early Work History
1960

In 1957, when I was fourteen, I went to work at Flowerwood Nursery in Loxley, which was run by my cousin, Bobby Duck. We started to work at 7:00 a.m. and worked until 5:00 p.m. Flowerwood would send a big labor truck with a canvas top through the community to pick up workers and take them back home. Trouble is, the turn-around point was three miles from my house, so I had to walk those miles to catch the truck in the mornings and again back home in the evenings, unless someone was at home who could drive me. And as it turned out, all the riders were black women. I was the only white person on the truck, but those old Negro women took a liking to that little scrawny white boy, and I enjoyed the ride. And I was earning a wage. My paycheck was $14.00 per week, less $.62 held out for taxes. And did I mention that we worked five full days plus a half day on Saturday? That was one summer. The next year, when I was fifteen, I worked at Beasley's Grocery store, and the two years after that, I worked at Baldwin Furniture Company as an appliance repairman helper. I did that until I graduated and moved to Mississippi to go to college.

A couple of interesting things happened while I was at Baldwin Furniture. I remember being called into work one Christmas Eve to help deliver stereos and other goodies to different houses around midnight, while everyone but the daddy of the house was asleep, so he could surprise his daughter with a gift on Christmas morning. So I got to play Santa Claus until way into the night. I was the assistant to Mr. James Thornton, who was the appliance serviceman. Now, James was a good guitar player and singer, and he did a lot of that on the side. James played and sang a lot with a guy named Hank Locklin. Eventually, the two of them had a chance to sign a contract and go on the road together. James decided that he did not want to leave his wife and family, so Hank went without James. You may have heard of Hank Locklin. He recorded several hits, one of which was "Love's Cheating Line.

Anyway, one day I was called out to the home of an older black woman who said her new Maytag washing machine wasn't working right; that the agitator would hardly turn at all. I went and checked it out. The trouble was – the lady did not have electricity in her home. So she strung together a number of six-foot interior extension cords and ran them from her neighbor's house, about one hundred feet away, to her front porch, where her washing machine was located. I bet she was not getting twenty watts of power. So I explained the problem to her and told her that if she moved her Maytag to her neighbor's porch and plugged it in, it would work just fine. She did, and it did.

One episode I recall as a serviceman was not quite so innocent. I went to a lady's house to work on her washing machine. I was crouched down behind it when she walked up. She was an attractive lady, probably in her early thirties, with a good figure, long hair, and a pretty face. She was wearing a very thin see-through negligee and stood so that it would open and show her legs. It was pretty obvious as to what she was inviting me to do. You have to remember, I was seventeen with raging hormones. It was a very unsettling situation for me, and frankly, I was scared half to death. I finished the job as fast as I could and got out of there. Thank God I did not give in and put myself in a dangerous predicament.

Chapter Sixteen
High School
1961

When I started High School in the seventh grade, I moved from Crossroads in the woods to Bay Minette in town. It was a big adjustment for me. Town people were different from the ya-hews I was used to in the country. Some of them looked down on us country hicks, and would not associate with us. But for the most part, I was just ignored by those of upper-crust status. And some of the town boys actually liked me because they wanted to visit my country home and experience the wonders and sounds of the wild. In the 7th grade, I was attacked by some kind of blood disorder that caused boils (we called them risins) to break out all over my body. At one time, I had thirty-four from my knees down. I had a huge one on the back of my wrist that was lanced by a doctor. I had one underneath my arm and passed out when a fellow student innocently grabbed me there. I came to in the Principal's office, who wanted to take me to the doctor. But I declined and told them I knew how to handle it. When I got home, Dad took me to the woods to help him saw trees with a two-man crosscut saw, and as I was sawing, the boil broke open and healed. To cure my blood disorder, the doctor prescribed some large tablets called Espotabs, and because I took so many so often, I was soon able to swallow them without water. But Espotabs were meant as a female treatment, and soon my breasts started growing, became extremely sore and sensitive, and began seeping liquid. I recall fishing with my dad one day when I was not wearing a shirt. Dad asked me if I had been smoking marijuana. I replied, "Not lately; why?"

And he said, "Well, your breasts are big for a man, and marijuana can cause that. I still have king-sized breasts. And I still do not know how my Dad knew about marijuana and breasts". I did not ask!

As far as school was concerned, I was an okay student, and made mostly B's on my report card, along with an occasional A. I remember crying at my first C in the ninth grade. I always took school seriously and did my best. I enjoyed English and Literature. We had an assignment in the ninth grade to write a poem. To me, it was a breeze, but to many of my classmates, it was a nightmare. So being the good friend I was, I offered to write poems for some of them, which I sold for a quarter a piece. But in the 10th grade, I was stricken with acute Bright's disease, a serious disorder of the kidneys, which caused me to miss forty-two consecutive days of school. At the time, I was taking Algebra II and typing. I got 70 pages behind in Algebra lessons, and recall my Mother staying up with me many nights until 2:00 a.m., helping me make up missed assignments. I passed Algebra with a "D" that year and got an "I" in typing, which was eventually changed to a "D". Only later did I learn that I had applied the formula that determined my typing grade incorrectly, so that "D" was really unearned.

I also participated in a program known as Diversified Occupations (D.O.), which allowed me to earn a credit by working one-half day at a public job. I took the job as the assistant to the appliance repairman at Baldwin Furniture Store, owned by Mr. Wayland Woodson. That is where I met Mr. James Thornton, whom I mentioned earlier. Anyway, I ended up being chosen as 'Mr. D.O.' my senior year, was elected as 1st Vice-President and got a 8x10 picture in the school yearbook.

Chapter Seventeen
Off to College
1961

I graduated High School in satisfactory style and was accepted for college by Troy University and William. Carey College (WCC). I was a big Crimson Tide fan, but I was deathly afraid of going to that giant university in Tuscaloosa. No way a country bumpkin like me was going to succeed there. Besides, I had no money and no scholarship. I had to work my way all through college. I remember my dear Mother paying $400 a year for the first two years, but the rest was up to me. As soon as I got to Hattiesburg, I got a job at Jim Bomboy's Appliance store as their service man. I went to school in the mornings and worked there in the afternoons. I also worked through the Christmas break, which meant I lived in a big dormitory all by myself for a couple of weeks. And I worked in the school cafeteria as a dishwasher and as a food server on the meal line. I moved up to jobs that were a bit classier later on, but I worked each of my four years there. I really wanted to go to Troy, but my sister's husband had graduated from WCC, and he took me to Hattiesburg, Mississippi, one weekend, and introduced me to the faculty and talked me into going there. It turned out that I enjoyed my time at Carey. I was a Hall-Proctor in my Sophomore year; I was the Sportswriter for the basketball and the baseball teams, and had my articles published in fourteen newspapers. I was employed by the Office of Public Affairs. I was Vice-President of my Senior Class; was the Co-Editor of the Lance, the Student Handbook, and was chosen for the Jenkins-Chestang Citizenship Award, the most prestigious honor of the college.

Chapter Eighteen
A Bellyful of Church
1961

I tole you thqt my parents were more religious than they were Christian. They were at church every Sunday morning, Sunday evenin Wednesday nights and any other time their was an church occasion., including work projects. Speaking of work projects, the church invited bids to clean the three-story wood building, and my dear ole Dad submitted a bid of $8.00 for the weekly job. Of course, he was the successful bidder, so my brother and I were privileged to sweep all three stories with a broom; to collect all trash and empty the trash cans; to scrape the chewing gum off the underside of the pews; and to rearrange the songbooks and Bibles that people had left out of place. All this for $8.00 per week. Oh, there was another project that my Dad successfully bid on. The four-acre cemetery next to the church needed mowing every other week, so Dad turned in a bid of $5.00. That's right – four acres; five dollars. That church kept us busy. I well remember sitting in the shade of a big oak tree when we took a lunch break, eating sardines, moon pies, and RC Colas.

Now, please note that I said my parents were 'religious'. They were also Christians, that is, believers in Jesus Christ, but they did not practice His love very well or very often. Together, they produced a total of seven births, five of whom made it to adulthood, plus one miscarriage. I guessed that they 'engaged' often, but they really did not like each other very much. They fussed a lot. Mother resented Daddy for keeping her barefoot and pregnant and in the kitchen. They had some major fusses when Mother decided to take a job in town. Daddy interpreted that as being unable to support his family, and it was an embarrassment to him. Another big fuss happened when I was seventeen years old, and Mother helped me buy my first automobile – a 1951 Ford - without telling Daddy first. I didn't get to keep that car very long. He traded it for a pickup truck. There was always a bone of contention between them.

When I was very young, I was not a ware of all of this, but as I entered my teenage years, it really started to bear on me. I could see a big difference in the way they lived at home and the way they presented themselves at church – especially my Dad. Actually, my Mother carried her attitude over into church. She would criticize people, sometimes openly and to their face. She would accuse other women of making a pass at Dad. The distance between them continued to grow to the point where she would not sit in the same room with him and would openly criticize and ridicule him. Her resentment grew as she got older, and at one time she made the remark, 'As far as I am concerned, you and your Dad are divorced.' But she would never have gone through with a divorce. Remember, that was one of those forbidden words. This strained relationship continued until my older sister, their firstborn, contracted cancer and was put in the hospital under hospice care. Then they started to talk politely to each other again and reconciled their differences. They were actually civil. My sister died from cancer at the age of fifty-five. But her husband remarked to me 'If her death was what it took to get them back together, the price was too damn high!'. Anyway, Mother had a heart attack three years later and died at the age of 78. Dad lived another eight years after her death, and he died when he was 98 years old.

55

Chapter Nineteen
College
1961

My job in the Public Affairs Office caused me to be known both on campus and in the community. One of my jobs was to visit the downtown merchants and 'invite' them to contribute to the financial well-being of the local institute of higher learning. I wrote a lot. Besides being the Sports Writer, and Co-Editor of the Student Handbook, I also had an article published in the school newspaper about a fatal automobile accident I witnessed firsthand, and watched two elderly people burn to death. Oh, and I taught Business Office Machines and Business English when the Professor was absent. It was fun.

William Carey College (now University) was, and is, a Baptist-supported school, and as such, it turned out a lot of what was known as 'Preacher Boys'; that is, Ministerial Students. I soon learned that the 'Preacher-boys' were no saints themselves. They did not always practice what they preached. See the next chapter.

It was at this Christian college that I learned to never blindly accept a person just because he happened to be a preacher. Some are good; probably most are. But some are not. I also got into a fight one time with a former preacher student who was visiting some friends. Right next door was a visiting missionary couple, and they reported the ruckus to the College Dean. Fighting meant automatic expulsion, so the next morning I was summoned to the Dean's office and questioned. I was truthful about it, and when I explained the reason for the fight, he told me to forget that it ever happened. Man, was I relieved.

58

Chapter Twenty
Sports – Not My Calling
1961

I always liked sports. I told you I was the Sportswriter in College. Trouble is, I was no good at playing sports at all. I did not have the build of an athlete. Even though I worked hard on the family farm, I never developed big muscles, and never put on any weight. I remember asking my Dad if I could go out for football in High School, and I thought he was going to whip me for asking. Instead, I got a half-hour lecture about how he could not afford to pay for me to play and how I was needed on the farm. But I did ask the football coach, and he told me "Harold, those guys would kill you out there". Shoot, I don't know why he said that; I weighed 115 pounds. So instead I sat in the stands every Friday night and watched my buddies play football. Then, in college, I played Intramural sports. I got two front teeth knocked out playing intramural football; I sprained my ankle attempting a lay-up in basketball and limped around on crutches for six weeks; and I got my face smashed, and my nose broken playing third base on the church softball team. For some unknown reason, I decided that was enough of participating in sports for me. Good thing the college needed a sportswriter.

Chapter Twenty-One
Can't Trust Those Preacher Boys
1962

I told you all of this to set the stage for later events and attitudes in my life. I graduated from High School in 1961 and applied to Troy University. I was accepted and was prepared to go when this brother-in-law I mentioned above persuaded me to go to William Carey College (now University) in Hattiesburg, Mississippi. I enrolled there and pursued a Bachelor of Science degree in Business Administration. Carey was a Baptist-supported school and turned out a lot of young preachers. I was the Sports Writer for the Basketball and Baseball teams and became friends with the athletes. Even though we, Business and Sport majors, did not associate with these 'preacher-boys' very closely, I did start noticing them and their way of living. Their lifestyle only supported and strengthened my teenage views of religion and Christianity. I knew preachers who smoked; who cussed; who drank'; who made indecent hand gestures; who were married but had girlfriends at the remote churches where they were a pastor. In fact, one of them was married to a good-looking redhead who liked boys, and he would lock her up in their apartment when he left to go preach so she could not entertain certain friends. This action just drove me further away from the pseudo-religion they practiced. In fact, in my rebellion, I started smoking cigarettes and drinking beer while at this Christian college.

Chapter Twenty-Two
Marriages
1964 – 1980

I excelled in Marriage almost as well as I did in sports. I have failed miserably at marriage, with the exception of my last wife, of course, which lasted forty-four plus years until her death. I have always liked girls and have always had a girlfriend since I was in the seventh grade. I had one special high school sweetheart during my Senior year, and at the time, no one could convince me that we would not be married as soon as she graduated. I recall her Father telling me, 'There's not one chance in a million that y'all are going to get married. In fact, if y'all do get married, I will give you some land and build you a house'. To me, that sounded great because I knew we were going to prove him wrong. But after graduation from High School, I moved 120 miles away to attend college. At first, I would drive home every weekend just to spend time with my heart-throb, but for some reason, my Mother did not want this relationship to succeed, so she suggested that I start spending weekends on the college campus. I did, and sure enough, the day came when my girlfriend and I parted ways. We will go through the first marriage and a couple more later on.

Chapter Twenty-Three
Marriage No. 1 – Big Mistake
1964

During my Senior year at Carey, I noticed a nice-looking lady who worked in the Admissions Office, and walked down there one day to ask her for a date. She was not in the office, but another girl was there, so I asked her out instead. She accepted, and later we started dating regularly. I did not know it at the time, but she had a boyfriend, and one day he showed up at my dorm room ready for a fight because I was dating his girlfriend. I told him. 'Shoot; take her back. She never told me she had a boyfriend.' But this girl's mother did not like the boyfriend, and she strongly encouraged her daughter to pursue our relationship. After we had been dating for several months, she told me that her Mother said we had to get married immediately. Her period was late, and she thought she might be pregnant. And her Dad was a pastor at a local church, and if she had a baby out of wedlock, it would cost him his job and his reputation. So we hurriedly got married. Being the 'good little boy' who did what he was told to do, that is what we did; one week later. Big mistake! No counseling, even though her Dad was a preacher; no praying; no thinking it through. We just got married because her mother said we had to. She was not pregnant. She and her Mother had concocted the whole deal to get her away from her former boyfriend. But it worked. She was married to me. After graduating from college, I joined the United States Air Force, and things got worse between us.

After we were married, my new bride moved into the house that my brother and I were renting. Well, she was a music major, and she was good at playing the piano, but she knew absolutely nothing about cooking, ironing, or cleaning house. She was never taught to do this kind of work when she was growing up.

One day, she tried to fry chicken and followed a recipe that called for rolling it in ground-up cornflakes. It was half raw. It was awful, but I bragged on it. But Dwight would not touch it. Speaking of chicken, one day I noticed a terrible smell in the kitchen. I tried to find the source, but couldn't, and it kept getting worse and worse, to the point we could hardly stand to be in there. So I kept digging around, and finally I found a whole chicken in the bottom kitchen cabinet, still in the grocery bag like it was when we bought it two weeks earlier. I pulled that thing out, put her in the car, told her to hold the bag, and drove us out into the country, where she flung it out the window. She was also not too industrious. She did not do much of anything except practice her music. When we visited my parents, she would crash on the couch and take a nap until it was time to go home. My Dad once told me that she was the laziest woman he had ever seen. Now, let me say something to you here. This marriage was a disaster from the start. It never should have happened. She was not pregnant. She and Mother concocted the whole story and conspired to trick me into marrying her. We were Christians, but we never prayed about it. We did not ask God if this was His will. Later on in life, I would be criticized and ostracized for being divorced, and quoted the scripture "What God has joined together, let not man put asunder". I know that verse as well as anyone, but God did not join us together. God had nothing to do with it. And I told those self-pious

Pharisees that sometimes what 'man had joined together, God had to put asunder'. We were never in love; we were never close; we never enjoyed each other's company; and we were not meant for each other.

While I was in the Air Force, I started drinking pretty heavily; had several girlfriends – some married; some single. One thing I learned during this time was the fact that there were numerous married women out there who enjoyed an adulterous relationship. There was no shortage, and believe me, I took advantage of that. After my discharge from the Air Force in 1970, the preacher's daughter and I got a divorce.

This marriage existed for nine years, four of which was in the Air Force, until it fell apart one year after I was discharged. Now, this lady was not an ugly person; she was a nice lady. She, as I, was not ready for marriage. We were much too young, immature, and inexperienced at 20 and 21 years old, and didn't know what to expect or how to deal with married life. But man, she could play the piano. I think she went on to a career in classical music, for which I am glad. Of course, our divorce brought that shame on her family and her preacher daddy, which he had feared years earlier. But we all survived. More to come!

Chapter Twenty-Four
My First Job
1965

When I graduated from college, I figured I was ready for the business world. After all, I had a Bachelor of Science degree in Business Administration. I was all set for a prestigious position as a manager of a corporation. I imagined how eager and receptive the CEO would be to accept my ideas and suggestions. Well, it didn't work out quite like I had planned or hoped for. The only job offer I got upon graduation was that of an outside sales rep for Capital Bolt and Screw Company, a wholesale corporation that sold industrial fasteners. So I hit the road every day, visiting our clients or prospective customers in hopes of selling them a bunch of nuts, bolts, screws, and washers. I kept that job for a year, and I guess I did okay. I remember one of my last sales was for high-tensile strength three-inch bolts and nuts to a military contractor who used them to anchor a tower in Vietnam. Oh, and I was the supervisor of the warehouse crew, which consisted of one older black gentleman named Fred, and Fred knew a lot more about the business than I ever would. We became good friends, and Fred taught me the ropes about the business. But I did learn one valuable lesson. The President of the company told me when he hired me that he would give me a pretty substantial raise in six months. At the end of six months, he called me into his office and explained that he could not give me a raise as promised because his bookkeeper made the same salary that I did, and that she would get mad if I were paid more than she was. So much for promises made – promises kept! And my salary is a whopping $6,600 per year. And even in 1965, that was nothing to brag about. I quit my job and joined the U. S. Air Force.

Chapter Twenty-Five
U.S. Air Force
1966

After quitting my job with the company that failed to keep its promise, I went to the recruiting office in Jackson, Mississippi, and joined the U.S. Air Force. I told the Recruiter that I wanted to be a test pilot, and of course, he readily agreed. Recruiters will promise you anything to get you to sign up. I took the written test and scored high on it. But after I had put my name on the line, I was told that I was not selected for Officer's Candidate School because the college I graduated from was not recognized by the Air Force. So I became an Enlisted recruit with a grade of E-1 (Basic) rather than a Second Lieutenant. I was offered several fields of study and chose Electronics. Actually, I asked about the Navy school, but was told that they required a six-year enlistment versus a four-year stint for the Air Force. I was not interested in a career with the military, so Air Force it was, and I was shipped off to Lackland AFB in San Antonio, Texas. That was in July 1966, and man, was it hot! There were several days when the Red flag flew, signifying a temperature of 120 degrees or above. The Red Flag meant all outdoor training was suspended. But we had two Drill Sergeants who did not believe in the Flag, so they ignored it and continued to conduct daily training. Overall, basic training was not too difficult. I had done more than most of our exercises when growing up on the farm and in the woods. But there were some city boys there who were not used to a military lifestyle or discipline, and two or three of them flunked out and were either sent home or forced to start over at day one.

I got hit in the stomach by one of those stern Drill Sergeants. We had just finished our mid-day chow and were milling around on the training pad while waiting for the drill instructors. It was extremely hot, and I took off my pith helmet to wipe my forehead. Now that was against the rules. I knew that, but I was sweating and wanted to wipe it off. Well, the instructor was just coming out of the chow hall, and he saw me. He never said a word. He just walked up to me and back-handed me in the belly. I thought I was going to throw up. It was not hard to dislike the training sergeants there. Shortly after we landed and were assigned to our barracks, we were taken to what we called the Green Elephant to receive our issuance of Government-Issued clothing. The Green Elephant was a huge metal consquent hut with no windows. It must have been at least 130 degrees inside there, and I was so thirsty that my tongue was sticking to the roof of my mouth. Suddenly, we walked past a water fountain, and following proper protocol, I politely requested permission for a drink from the fountain. The training instructor said, "Sure, Airman Duck. Help yourself." I was overjoyed at the thought of a drink of cool water and made a beeline for the fountain. But just as I pushed the button for water, the instructor reached behind it and turned off the valve. Then he said, rather sarcastically and loud enough for everyone to hear, "Now get back in line, Airman Duck, and don't buck the program again!" I want to tell you something; I didn't know I could hate someone that much. If I had had a gun, I think I could have killed him right there on the spot. Then we got all our vaccinations. We were in a line, and there were two medics, one on either side of the line. Each had an air gun, and they popped us in each arm as we passed by. You had to lean into the air gun to keep from getting cut. One of the recruits pulled away, and he got a huge gash down his arm, pouring blood. The medics never said a word and never bandaged the cut. A lot more of that kind of stuff happened, but I am sure you are tired of reading about it. You get the point. We were not treated with respect, to say the least.

Chapter Twenty-Six
First Assignment –
1966 Keesler AFB, Mississippi

I graduated from Boot Camp after six weeks and was granted a short leave from duty. This is funny. I enlisted in the Air Force, weighing 183 pounds. I had long hair. I was wearing mod civilian clothes. After six weeks of boot camp, I came out weighing 157 pounds; had a skint haircut, and had on a starched Khaki uniform complete with a hat and visor. I walked up to my wife, and she did not recognize me at all. I had to tell her, look at me, it's me! After leaving, I was sent to Keesler AFB in Biloxi, Mississippi, for Electronics school. I excelled there and was placed in the accelerated course, finishing a one-year study in seven months. Since I was married, I was allowed to live off-post. I rented a little cabin that was situated behind one of those massive Antebellum homes in Biloxi. Our rental unit had one bedroom, a kitchen, a small living room, a small bath, and a screen porch. And I paid $45.00 a month for it, including utilities. My pay from the Air Force was $87.00, so rent took over half of my income. In 1969, Hurricane Camille completely demolished the big house and my little bungalow.

One day, while we were on the drill pad, the Sergeant walked up behind me and yelled, "Don't you know how to march, Airman? You walk more like a duck than you do an Airman!' Not to be outdone, I retorted, "That's because I have been a Duck a lot longer than I have been an Airman. That made him mad, so he told me to fall out of formation and go to a small drill pad. Then he told one of the cadets to march me for two hours, and he went back to the squadron to finish their drill. As soon as he was gone, the intermediate helper told me, "Hey, just walk around for a little while to make him think you are marching."

Chapter Twenty-Seven
Shaw AFB, South Carolina
1967

From Keesler, I went to Shaw AFB in Sumter, South Carolina, and became part of a team that repaired and maintained electronic equipment for the aircraft there, mostly Phantoms F-4C and F-15 Fighter jets. Our mobile home was at the end of the flight line, and when they fired up those humongous planes, our dishes would actually slide across the table Once I was honored as Airman of the Month, only to be reprimanded by the top Sergeant for wearing a uniform with a hole in the pants leg. Hey, at least they were starched and ironed. Shortly afterward, moving to the trailer park, I was visited by an attractive lady who told me about a 'wife-swapping' club and asked me if I wanted to join. I told her, "Hey, sounds good to me, if I can talk my wife into it." Well, the wife didn't like the idea very much, so we never joined. I don't know if I would have actually done it or not.

While at Shaw in 1967, our Flight was on stand-by alert to deploy to Israel for their war with Egypt, but by the time we got packed and ready to go, Israel had already won the Six-Day War. Soon afterwards, our Flight of 39 Airmen got orders to go to Vietnam. We were sent to the backwoods of Eglin AFB for combat, capture, torture, and survival training. Believe me, it was much more intense and difficult than was our basic training. Our day started at 0500 and ended at 2100. We 'double-timed' everywhere we went; we never walked. We had hand-to-hand combat training; hand grenade training; we went on forced marches at 0200 hours; we ran an obstacle course four times a day. We crawled through black dirt under live fire – or so we were told. No one ever challenged it. We had search and destroy exercises and survival training. We were dropped off in a remote area on a survival exercise with nothing but a compass, and were told to find our way back to camp, while being ambushed by snipers. The exercise lasted three days, and we were given nothing to eat. We had a roll-up pup tent for the nights, but no food or water. We started out eating berries we found along the way, and some of the guys tried grasshoppers and other insects. One day, we came upon a small stream, and we all filled our canteens. Then I took out the little emergency sewing kit we had been given; used the thread for a fishing line; bent a safety pin into a hook; and caught a lizard for bait. Then I went fishing. I did not catch a fish, but I did hook a turtle and used my helmet for a pot and made turtle soup. The guys almost beat me up to get some of it. We ate the legs and drank the broth. I think I got maybe two bites. Then just as the base camp came into sight, I got 'killed' by a sniper. They really put us through it. But we realized what was ahead of us and knew it was necessary for our survival in Nam.

One day, while in training indoors, one of the guys sat down in his chair and ignited a bomb. The instructor yelled, "Congratulations, Soldier! You just blew up the entire squad. You stupid idiot! Always check underneath your chair before you sit down." My brother Dwight was already in DaNang at the time, and the only bright spot in my training was that I might be stationed there with him. But before we received our deployment orders, twelve of the thirty-nine Airmen at our station were put on hold while the Security Command did an investigation, and they froze the orders to

Vietnam and conducted a very thorough investigation of our past. The FBI or CIA sent agents to the middle of nowhere in Crossroads, Alabama, to ask my neighbors about my character and past. They thought I was in serious trouble; they did not know what kind of crime I had committed against the United States. When it was over, the Army chose six of the twelve to transfer from the Tactical Air Command to the Security Command. I was one of those six, was given a Top-Secret Clearance by the military, and was sent to advanced electronic schools.

I was first stationed at Ft, Devens, Massachusetts, and then at Goodfellow AFB in San Angelo, Texas, before being sent overseas. Believe me, it was cold in Massachusetts, and our facility was at the top of a steep hill. The guys who were locals would slide down the hill as if they were skiing, and would laugh at me for falling. While I was at Ft Devens, I met a guy from New Hampshire. We both were assigned to Goodfellow AFB and became friends. The four used to go to stock car races each Friday, Saturday, and Sunday nights. He, I, and his wife enjoyed it, but my wife was not interested. One night, as we were playing cards at our house, I felt the foot of my friend's wife make its way up my pants leg. I gave her a surprised look, and she smiled sweetly. From there, our friendship grew until it went far beyond the point it should have.

Chapter Twenty-Eight
Karmursel, Turkey
1969

After graduating from the electronics school at Goodfellow, I was deployed to Karamursel, Turkey, instead of Vietnam. I landed there on my twenty-sixth birthday. When I was sent to Turkey, so was my friend, and he decided to move his wife there as well, so our friendship picked up where it had left off. We worked swing shifts there; four days, four evenings, four mids, and four days off. One day, when I was working days, and my friend was working swings (from 4:00 p.m. to midnight), his wife invited me down to their house, which was eighteen miles from the base. So I caught the 5:00 p.m. bus and went to pay her a visit. I thought we were in for a good night of fun, but for some reason, she decided not to engage. So we talked until close to midnight, at which time I left and walked to the bus station. I had to hide while her husband dismounted the bus and then make a run for it to go back to the base. Well, I wasn't quick enough and the bus left without me. The next bus was scheduled for 5:00 a.m. So I sat at the bus stop in an unsafe neighborhood and shivered in the cold for five hours. You know what? I never had the desire to see that woman again. What a lesson!

I was in Turkey for almost one year. Our mission there was to intercept all radio transmissions from Russia; record them on tape; and send them to the CIA's Top-Secret mission. I was assigned as a repairman of the ground radio equipment. One night, while I was working on an oscilloscope, I got hit with four thousand volts. Thank goodness not with many amps. I had unplugged it, but forgot to drain a capacitor, which remained fully charged until I touched it. It knocked me about ten feet across the room. It hurt a lot then, but I had no lingering repercussions from it. I never told a soul about that incident.

While I was in Turkey, I pretty much forgot about God and had fun. I drank way too much. I used to send my brother audio tapes while he was in Vietnam, and he would promptly write to our mom and dad saying he got another tape from me, and again, I was drunk. I recall getting into a fight with a friend who paraded me back through the bar, covered with mud from head to foot, in front of all my buddies. Then I went to the barracks and enjoyed a 'commode-hugging' drunk. Crazy!

I was not the only crazy person in Turkey. Remember the friend who beat me up? He asked me one day if I would entertain his wife that night so he could go visit his girlfriend. So I took his pickup truck, picked up his wife, and we drove to the top of a small hill overlooking the compound and talked. That's all. Just talked. She told me she knew about the girlfriend and she knew that her husband had asked me to 'baby-sit' her while he was away. She was not mad about it, but I really felt sorry for her.

Chapter Twenty-Nine
My Discharge
1970

The drinking continued. A few of us drank while on the flight to McGuire AFB, where I was discharged, and then on the subsequent flight to Atlanta. It was about four in the morning, and not many people were on the plane. We were in uniform, and the stewardess flirted with us. I enjoyed that plane ride. I flew into Mobile and caught a ride to the Greyhound bus station, where my parents came to pick me up about eight o'clock. I was still pretty much hungover at the time, but Dad wanted me to drive his new car home, so I did, weaving and wobbling. Dad blamed it on the uneven ruts in the pavement, but my dear ole Mom knew the reason. Bless her heart. I really put her through some grief. By the grace of God, we made it.

Just prior to my discharge, I was recruited for re-enlistment and was told I had been selected for Officer's Candidate School. I said "No, Thanks". I wanted to be a civilian again. After my discharge, I was under a gag order that prohibited me from discussing my duties there for seven years. But looking back, I think I would have enjoyed a life as a military officer. Instead, I became a Veteran with my military service complete. Little did I know that I would spend another twenty-one years with the U. S. Army.

Chapter Thirty
Mortgage Banker
1970

After I was discharged in 1970, I enrolled in Graduate School at the University of Southern Mississippi. But the Veterans Administration messed up my paperwork, so I quit after one quarter due to lack of money and looked for a job. I put out my resume in Mobile, Alabama, and Jackson, Mississippi, and was offered a job by a Mortgage Banking firm in Jackson. Here is a funny side note to my hiring. I was interviewed by the Secretary of the Company. He liked me and took me to meet the President. The President talked to me for a while, and then he asked me, "You are from Alabama. If we give you a job and invest our money to train you, how do I know you will not leave us and go back to Alabama?" I replied, "Sir, I promise you I will be loyal to Mississippi and to your company until football season starts, but there is no way I am going to pull against the Crimson Tide." The President smiled, and told the Secretary "Hire him!" I was later told that the President was not only from Alabama, but he was a graduate of the University of Alabama. When I was hired, I was given the title of Assistant Secretary and made a supervisor of five ladies. I studied hard, learned the business, and was promoted to Vice-President after two years, and was Supervisor of the largest division in the company. I kept that job for six years and really enjoyed it. I grew the department from five to twenty-three people, mostly young girls from rural areas who came to the Capital City in the big town to get a good job. Trouble was, these attractive young girls were aspiring and accommodating and not adverse to doing favors to a Vice-President in charge of hiring. I hate to admit it now, but at the time, the young Vice-President was pretty accommodating too. It was fun then, but I am not proud of it now.

As Vice-President, I had a good life. I had a good salary. I had a private office, a private conference room, two secretaries, a company car, a membership in the local Country Club, and unlimited authority. Life was good. My department was responsible for, among other things, maintaining the bank accounting records of thirty-eight investors; some small and easily done; some very large, complex, and difficult. The lady who worked for me, who was responsible for balancing these accounts each month, became unable to keep them up to date. When I learned of it, I pitched in to help her and balanced several of them. I recall working all night one time, with only a two-hour nap on the office floor. Unfortunately, we had an audit before all the corrections were made, and two of the large investors demanded some changes. The President of the company called me in one day, and with tears in his eyes, he told me, "Sport, these two financial giants that are our clients have demanded that we take some drastic action to correct the inefficiencies that the auditor found, and I hate like the dickens to do this to you, but you are the scapegoat." So I lost my good, high-paying job and started looking for another job.

Chapter Thirty-One
Marriage No. 2 – The Wild Side
1973

After nine years of an unhappy relationship, I was ready to move on. But I wanted no part of a preacher, or religion, or church, or being chided for a divorce. The preacher daddy of my first wife was one of those guys who thought the world owed him special favors because he was a 'Man of God'. He would ask for discounts at every store he went to; he would ask for contributions to carry on his ministry; he would canvass the community, begging people for donations. All of this really turned my stomach. Remember, I grew up working hard and earning everything I got. I did not beg, and I did not respect those who did.

And then there was the pseudo-religion of people like my parents, who appeared so religious but could not stand each other. So I rebelled. I did like Esau in the Bible, who married a couple of Canaanite women just to spite his parents.

I met a woman who was as anti-church as I was. She liked to drink, party, and go to the honky-tonks. That suited me fine because I had had it with religious folks. This woman filled the bill. She liked to drink and dance and smoke cigarettes and have a good time. We hit it off. Trouble was, she had a husband, and I had a wife. So we both got divorces, and we went to the Justice of the Peace and said 'I reckon I will' and married each other. For a while, it was fun. We went to bars often; we went to parties; we got drunk; we went to ballgames. We made good money, and we built a new house, and bought a few new cars. One of the vehicles was a customized van with captain chairs, a sink, an ice box, and a sofa that made a bed. It was nice, and we used it to transport our friends to the parties and ballgames. Life was fun, and we were on top of the world. We had tons of new friends as long as we footed the bill. But after a few years, things began to unravel. Life in the fast lane was not as much fun as it first was. And we were wasting a lot of money. We started fussing a lot. We lived in a dangerous world. Once, a guy who thought I was pursuing his wife (I wasn't) stuck a gun up to my head and told me he was going to blow me away. I told him to have at it, but instead he cussed me out and left. We were both drunk at the time. He called the next morning to apologize. I told him that I did not want his apology and did not want to ever see him again. And I didn't. Another time I pulled up beside a car load of young people at a traffic signal and pointed my pistol at them just to watch them dive to the floorboard in fear. Then I drove off.

I reached the point where I wanted to drink less, but my wife did not. In fact, she sometimes had a drink of vodka before she went to work in the mornings. She did not like my parents (the feeling was mutual; they did not have much respect for her either), and she hated to visit them. When we did go, which was very infrequently, she would put a bottle of vodka or gin in that customized van, and while I drove to my parents' home, she would get boozed up. So I always told them she was sick when we were there. In fact, when our relationship first started, my family did not know where I lived; they had no address for me, and no phone number. The only way they could communicate with me was by writing to my post office box. It was not a very good time in my life. It started out fun, but it ended up disastrous. That marriage lasted seven years. And in those seven years, God was nowhere to be found in my life. I never attended church nor had any desire to do so.

This break from church and right living lasted for nearly ten years. Sometimes it was fun; sometimes it was not. My wayward wife and I got into scuffles or outright fights. Slowly, the wicked side of life began to disturb me. My wife was drinking more than ever. Sometimes she would have a slug of gin before she went to work. We fought more and more. I never hated her; in many ways, she was a good person. She just could not control her drinking. Both of her parents were alcoholics.

Now let me tell you how this story ends. I came home one day after work, and I did not feel well. I had a fever and felt like I was catching the flu. I just wanted to go to bed. But my wife wanted to go 'juking,' and she got mad. While I was asleep, she woke me up by putting out a cigarette on my upper lip. I knew right then it was time for us to part ways. And we did. That's when I moved out of our house, never to live with her again. That was in the Spring of 1980.

Finally, I decided that this was not the kind of life I wanted and that I couldn't take it anymore. We got a divorce.

One last note on this marriage. This wife had a two-year-old son when she left with her husband, and when the two of us got married. The little boy really liked me, and I liked him too. We only saw him on weekends or every other weekend when he visited us. After seven years or so, when the marriage got rocky, I took him with me to cut wood for the fireplace. He was eight years old at the time. When I took a moment to rest, we were sitting on the tailgate of my pickup together, he asked me, "Daddy, are you and Mama gonna get a divorce?" and I replied, "Well, buddy, it sure looks that way", and he told me, "When y'all do, I wanna live with you". Man, that really tore my heart. I hugged him, cried, and explained that it would be impossible. I also gave him a .410 gauge shotgun that my Dad had bought for me when I was about twelve years old. Before I gave it to him, I removed the butt-plate, wrote him a note, and stuck it in the hollowed part of the stock. I think it was about forty years later, my nephew mentioned him, so I told him to ask if he still had that shotgun. He came back and told me that he still had it, so I told him to remove the butt-plate and retrieve my note. He did. He read it and made a copy, which my nephew emailed to me. But I never heard from him afterwards. I was later told that his mother had bad-mouthed me pretty badly to him, and he had no interest in contacting me. I understand that he has an important job with the U.S. Government, is happily married, and has two grown children. I am glad of that.

Chapter Thirty-Two
The Bee Lake Cabin
1975

I built a cabin on Bee Lake outside of Thornton, Mississippi. It was a nice house; three bedrooms; living room; kitchen; and a huge scrreened in porch across the back. I had a couple of boats there and I really enjoyed ruj8ng up and down the lake. My Mother came to visit one time and I took her across the lake to the grocery store. When we got ready to return to the cabin, the motor failed to start so I had to paddle us back home. My brother and his wife visited pretty often as well. We really had some good times there. He and his wife visited pretty often too. I remember one winter I went there to make sure the pipes did not freeze and my friend who owned a camp two lots down from mine asked me to check his too. Well, just as walked aroumd tp the backside a pipe exploded right at my feet and I jumped sky high. It sounded like a twelve-gauge shotgun blast. Back to Henry, I sold him the place when we left Mississippi and moved to Alabama. Later, Henry sold it to another guy and I heard that he burned it for insurance money. That made me sad because I had put a lot of time and work into it and it was a pretty place. I know that I built it almost single-handly. I would drive up sixty miles there and work almost all night. One night, around two o'clock in the morning, I was installing a new kitchen floor when a broom that was leaning against the wall fell due to the vibration of my hammer. I caught a glimpse of it as it fell and then heard the loud thump right beside me when it hit the floor. I had no idea what it was, and it scared me half to death. But we had fun at that lake house. We spent a lot of weekends there, and used to run trot-lines for catfish regularly. One day, I pulled up a huge catfish head only to find that an alligator had eaten the rest of it. Anyway, I sold out to Henry when we made out move to Alabama.

Chapter Thirty-Three
Mississippi Housing Authority
1976-1982

Shortly after leaving my job at the mortgage company, I got a call from the Director of the local Housing and Urban Development Office (HUD) office. He had been told that I was knowledgeable in the housing business and that I was available. Actually I was recommended by the wife of my friend Henry, who was the Secretary to the Director. I went in for an interview and was hired on the spot. But there was a stipulation. The program was known as the Section 8 Housing Program where residents would pay a portion of their rent based on a formula determined by their income and family size. We were to submit a list of clients under the program to HUD and HUD would send money to our office and, in turn, we would pay the landlord on behalf of the tenants. So the Government funded the program on the Federal level but it was administrated in the private sector through our office and governed by a Board of Commissioners. The money was available but there was no avenue for its application. An office had to be established and organized and then an application could be filed for its operation. It had been tried twice before, but the application was denied on the first try and the applicant embezzled the money and ran at the second attempt. So HUD was looking for a person to put it together from scratch. There were six counties in Central Mississippi and each county had a Commissioner, so I would be governed by a six-member Board. I met with the Board and got approved for the job. But no money could be passed until the organization was approved and in operation. So I was told that I would have to work without pay for three months while I completed and filed the very enormous and complicated application. Well, I did not have a job, so I took their offer and started filling out countless pages of Governmental questionnaires.

The Board agreed to a salary of $18,000 which was common in 1976. I worked long and diligently on that stack of papers, and finally finished it within the three month time-frame. I submitted it to HUD and was given authority to proceed, but for a salary of only $14,000, not the $18,000 we had agreed on. So I told the Board that I would take the $14,000 with the understanding that if I had done a suitable job, I would get the $18,000 in six months. (Reminded me of my job with Capital Bolt and Screw back in 1965). After the approval, I secured office space; wrote Job descriptions, Travel Policies; Acquisition Policies; Disposal Policies; and published job announcements; interviewed applicants; and hired and trained a staff.

I visited the local County Administrators and explained how it could benefit their economy and help solve the homeless situation. In addition I contacted private owners of rental properties and explained how it would ensure that they would receive the majority of their rent money on time each month. We started out with zero units of course, and I don't recall how many we had at the end of six months, but we were very successful. So I reminded the Board of Commissioners about our prior arrangement on salary and they approved the $18,000 as agreed. Now HUD got mad; they did not want me to get a raise because my salary would be higher than some of their personnel who worked this project. But HUD did not have the authority to deny it, so I got my increase. This started a riff between HUD and me that lasted until my last day on the job. What is that old saying? "You can't fight City Hall"? Well, you can't fight the Federal Government either and I got on their hit list. They actually had a small plane fly over and take pictures of my house and my vehicles to establish that I was living above my means, and that I had to be on the take from the property owners.

In the meantime, our organization grew more and more successful and we expanded from six counties to nine counties and from six Commissioners to nine. We started with zero units under contract and ended up six years later with over 2,100 privately owned houses and apartments under lease. We also promoted the construction of six new apartment complexes with over 900 units. So we were doing great, and even though HUD was mad, they could not deny our success. We soon became the second largest program in the State of Mississippi. But with our program, as is the case of any Federally funded program, there was abuse. We had tenants who claimed more children than they really had. We used to call them 'yard kids' because they were passed down the street from one tenant to the next. So we had people claiming six kids when they really had only two or three. Plus an application would show a single mom when in fact a live-in boy friend was staying there. In most cases, this live-in partner would have a job and an income that was not counted. In one such case, I had an employee sit outside and record the man friend leaving for work in the morning and returning that afternoon. I found out that his clothes were in her closet and that he received his mail at that address. I brought these things to the attention to the HUD officials but they never took any action and I was made the bad guy, accused of mishandling the program.

So all my complaining to HUD went unnoticed and just caused them to add more things that made me out to be a trouble maker, going against the grain. So we just turned a blind eye and continued to do our job.

I think we had about twelve employees if I remember correctly. Things rocked on smoothly without a hitch until two things happened. Here is the first one.

First I got a notice from HUD that they would be performing an audit on our program in two days. Normally, an audit would be annually with a two month warning to have time to get things in order and adjust personnel schedules. But ours would be in two days. Now here is the kicker: without my knowledge, of course, HUD had approached two of my employees; two I considered among my best; and convinced them to make up files on five fictitious houses and make rental payments each month to a landlord that did not exist. I will tell you the rest of the story in just a minute. So the HUD auditors showed up with briefcases in hand and the first five files that they pulled to review were the very files that had been fabricated by my employees. Of course when they investigated, they found out that they were false and made it appear that I had forged them and put the money in my pocket. I knew it was a bald-face lie and so did they, but their audit report said I was under suspicion of embezzlement. And they turned it over to the FBI, who interviewed my staff, and my employees in turn told me. When I got word of it, I called the FBI agent who was working the case, and said to him "I am told that you are asking questions about me. Do you want me to come to your office and answer them directly?" He said "I sure do"and I spent two hours being questioned by him. After it was all over, he wrote a report saying that he was satisfied that I did not know about it and that I was not guilty of doing anything wrong. This did not please HUD and they just closed the file on it. The auditors just suddenly left my office. I never got a report of the findings of their audit. It was just dropped from the scene – by HUD but not by me! As far as HUD wwas concerned, the matter was over. But not with me! I checked our records and got the post office box number in a neighboring city where the checks were being mailed. I went there; introduced myself; told then I was the Executive Director and I need to know the names on the P.O. Box. They told me and I headed right back to the office and called these two employees into my office. To my surprise, they came clean about being recruited by HUD. At the end of the day, those two good employees did not work for me anymore. You know what? After this, there was no mention about me or anyone else embezzling $25,000 from the program. It never made the local news and was not ever followed up on by anyone, especially from HUD because they are the ones who orchestrated it in the first place. I guess the money was refunded into the bank account and I suspect these two employees were re8nstated after my dismissal.

But I was not through making HUD mad at me. Here is the big Number Two! We had a statewide convention in Meridian and I was one of the featured speakers. When I gave my talk, I told the audience of over 300 that I did not like the program; that is was severely abused; that our success was counted by the number of people we had on welfare, and that instead of encouraging people to depend on the Government for their living, we should be teaching them how to become independent and support themselves. A total of five people out of three hundred told me afterwards that they agreed with me and commended me on having the courage to stand up and say it. You can imagine how well that went over with the HUD officials. That was the final nail in the coffin for me. So the HUD big-shots went into their secretive mode of operation. First, they appointed two new Commissioners to replace two of my friends and supporters. Now it had always beenthe practice in the past to move the Vice Chairman into the Chairman;s position at the end of a term. But that did not happen this time and the Vice-Chairman who was passed over, got up and walked out of the meeting, and the two new Commissioners who were appointed by HUD came on board; one of whom was announced as the new Chairman. Then HUD called a secret meeting without my knowledge of all my Commissioners, including these two new ones, and told them: "We do not have the authority to fire Harold outright, but you do and we want you to do it without delay. And if you do not do it, we do have the authority to defund the program and we will do that immediately and let the Program dry up and make you the bad guys to all the people who are participants under it." Well, the Commissioners called a special meeting with me and told me everything HUD had said. Three or four had tears in their eyes as they told me 'We are so sorry, but we really do not have a choice; we have to let you go." So I lost yet another job. Then they paid me three months salary as an entitlement, which HUD did not like, but could do nothing about it. Talk about scheming and underhanded methods. Again, without my knowledge HUD had already hired a new Executive Director who took my job on the very next day. I learned that the Government can be a crooked organization.

So HUD got the outcome tht they wanted and I was out. It was then that I took a job at Vegas Homes in Yazoo City.

Chapter Thirty-Four
My Buddy Henry
1979

But my wayward wife and I did have some good times along the way. It was during that time that I met a guy named Henry, who was married to the sister of my wife. Henry was an interesting guy. He was the son of a preacher, but as often happens, when he became a teenager, he decided he did not need religion or God, and he lived on the wrong side of the tracks for many years. He was tall, dark, slim, and handsome. He liked cars, and had some real classic ones. He always modified them and added his personal touch to make them stand out. He caught the eye of many a girl, and he knew how to show them a good time. He liked to drink back then, and he liked to fight. It didn't take much to set off his trigger temper. Most of that side of Henry had played out by the time I met him. But not altogether. I recall he bought a stripped-down van, which he immediately customized. He put in a plywood floor and covered it with carpet; he cut round portholes in each side; he installed captain chairs, an icebox, and a sofa seat. Then he painted it brown. It was nice when he finished, and we (the four of us) took several trips in it. One weekend, we went to Gulf Shores, Alabama, and spent the night in the State Park. Someone lit up a joint and passed it around. Suddenly, there was a knock on the van door, and there stood a County Sheriff. He looked at us, and then apologized. He said he thought we might be a bunch of kids down there smoking pot, but he could see that we were not teenagers. Then he told us to have a good night and drove away. We escaped jail that night.

One day, Henry was driving that same van down Highway 90 in Biloxi, Mississippi. He was pulling a small trailer and was driving in the left (fast) lane. A car pulled up on the right side beside us and told Henry to drive in the right lane. That did not sit well with Henry, and he yelled some stuff back at him and told him that he would drive wherever he liked. Then the guy pulled out his police badge, and I persuaded Henry to change lanes. Henry was not as wild as he once I was, but he did not like to be told what to do.

Another time I needed to move some stuff. I had a small trailer but no trailer hitch. I had a car, not a pick-up, so I went to a U-Haul dealership to rent a hitch, but it had already closed for the day. Then I noticed a rack holding some trailer hitches, so I just helped myself to one. The next day, the U-Haul manager called the cops and reported the stolen hitch. I told Henry about it, and he told me not to worry about it. I was scared of getting arrested, but Henry told me to give him the hitch. I did, and he promptly drove it to the U-Haul company and told them he found it on the side of the road and thought it may belong to them. They thanked him. End of story.

Another time, Henry borrowed one of my rifles. When he returned it, I found out that he had traded my rifle for a .38 caliber pistol. He never asked me if I wanted the trade. So I don't have my rifle, but I still carry that pistol to this day.

Henry was also hired in a supporting role for a couple of movies, and he met a lot of important movie stars, although I cannot recall who. Later, Henry came back to God. He wrote a book called 'This Is My Story; This Is

My Song', which is the story of his life. I have an autographed copy. Henry was quite a character, and I sure enjoyed our time together. I also liked his wife, Nelda, a lot. She was a better person than Henry or me. She put up with a lot! Bless her heart!

Henry was a good bass singer, and he joined a Gospel quartet and sang with them for several years.

Chapter Thirty-Five
Marriage No. 3 - God's Marriage
1980

After sixteen years of wasted life, I was alone again. I was far gone and well on the path of destruction, even with a remote connection to the underground mafia. I began to become convinced about living like that and about how I was not pleasing God,

There was a lady who was happily married to a man, and this man was a business associate of mine. He told his wife about me, and my past disasters with marriage, and his wife told her cousin, 'There is someone I want you to meet.' So her husband and my friend arranged for the two of us to meet. We did, and immediately started sharing backgrounds and failures and belief in God and straying so far from Him. We liked each other a lot, and we started dating.

She was a very nice, pretty, small lady with a background very similar to mine. She grew up in the country and attended church regularly. She had married a guy in the Air Force shortly after she graduated from High School and had moved to Nebraska. She had a daughter while they were living there. After his discharge, they moved back to Mississippi. One day, she came home from work early and found him in their bed with a prostitute. So that marriage ended. By the way, this guy sang in a Gospel quartet. By the way, he and my friend Henry were friends.

So now she was divorced and was lonesome. Not only that, she needed help raising a daughter. She met a man who appeared to be a decent person, and after dating him for a brief time, she married him out of desperation. But he was an alcoholic just like my second wife was, and he was mean to her and to her daughter. Once in a fit of anger, he decided to kill her and choked her until she passed out. Luckily for her, they were in the front yard at the time, and a neighbor came to her rescue. She came to her senses, and she divorced him. Man! Two marriages; two disasters. Just like me!

This lady and I had a good time dating each other. We would meet in the park for lunch and eat tomato sandwiches. I took her to the clothing store and bought her a pair of blue jeans – size Zero! She invited me over to her house for a steak dinner. Bless her heart; she fried it on the top of the stove as you would fry a pork chop and served it with butterbeans. I bragged on it like crazy, but I thought, I have to teach this woman how to grill a steak and bake a potato.

After we had dated for about eight or nine months, we decided to get married. When we got serious, we had a nice, big two-story house built in Florence, Mississippi, and we got married in our new house. Both sides of our families attended and were extremely happy that both of us had gotten rid of the no-good partners that we had before. Each of us was immediately accepted as a part of the other's family. That was on August 23, 1980. What a blessing! What a rescue by a loving and caring God who was watching over us. He was disappointed in us, I feel sure, but He did not give up on us. One man told me, 'God not only saw that you were worth saving; He also saw you were worth salvaging'. And that is what He did. I have absolutely no doubt that He put this lady in my life to save me from a horrible life and a terrible disaster.

We had been married less than a month when my new wife said, 'We need to get right with God again and change our way of living.' I was all for it, and we did. We found a good little country church and started attending. We met a lot of good and decent friends. We were not perfect, but they loved us and took us in as friends.

My new bride had an eleven-year-old daughter who had experienced a life of turmoil, abuse, and danger, and she liked me from the start. She would sneak around behind her mama's back and call me to tell me what she was doing, or cooking, and send me a picture of her. She was glad to have me as a caring and loving step-father. She had witnessed her mother's former husband choke her Mom until she passed out and been a victim of other cruel actions.

I cannot tell you how many times I have thanked the good Lord for sending Carolyn my way and causing her to influence my decisions. Given the fast-track life I was living before she came along, I have absolutely no doubt that I would either be dead or in prison today. Carolyn was a God-send to rescue me. God is merciful; He is long-suffering; and He is loving. I am a true-life example of that. That was in 1980, and He is still blessing me today. Hey, sometimes we disagree, but we have never doubted that this marriage had, and still has, God's blessing. And I will tell you this; it is a much calmer, sweeter, satisfying life than all the booze and partying and prowling. Nothing in this world could pull me back into that life style again.

Carolyn is a very special person. She has a heart for other people. I always said if she loved me as much as she loves her friends, I would be on top of the world. She is always cooking and inviting people over for a meal, or, at times, cooking and delivering meals to them. (She just did it again today as I was writing this paragraph). She loves entertaining guests, especially during the time of Christmas and other holidays. I don't even try to keep track of what she is doing; I just buy the food, fire up the grill, and shake hands with whoever happens to show up that day.

She is also an excellent interior decorator and has done numerous homes for friends. Many times, I have encouraged her to get her license and a bond and go into business, but she prefers to do it for her friends out of the kindness of her heart. My sister said Carolyn could take an out-house and make it look like a parlor. In 2007, when I bought my Dad's old dilapidated house and restored it, she had a ball decorating the interior. It looked like a Bed and Breakfast. In fact, it was nominated for Better Homes and Gardens and for Southern Living as a feature home. Neither of them ever did it, but it was an honor to be nominated.

And another passion of hers is flowers and birds. We must have had two dozen bird feeders in our back yard, and would sit for hours watching them. And I can't tell you how many flowers we have planted. Each time she goes to Lowe's or to the Country Wagon, she comes home with another bunch of flowers. One other thing, and I will shut up about her. She loves animals, and she dotes on a little Maltese-Yorkie mix dog that lives with us. If Blondie doesn't want her food, Carolyn will scoop it up and hand-feed her until it is all gone. I don't do too much except to give her a shower every week and walk her twice a day so she can take care of business.

Chapter Thirty-Six
Wives and Mothers-In-Law
1964-2007

It is a funny thing. I remember the day of my marriage to Carolyn very well, as if it were yesterday. I remember everyone who was there, and I remember Carolyn walking down the stairs from the second floor of our brand new house. But I remember very little about my first marriage. I recall the little church, and I remember my brother standing by me as my best man, but I do not remember getting nervous about seeing my bride-to-be walking down the aisle. I don't recall her stunning beauty or what she was wearing or our honeymoon or anything else. Oh, I do remember that we went to visit my sister in Missouri. That was our honeymoon. And as far as marriage number two goes, I recall even less. We went to the Justice of the Peace, and it was an in-and-out ordeal that took only a few minutes.

But I remember all three of my Mothers-in-Law. Mother-in-Law number one was the wife of a preacher, and he was not a handyman. In fact, he could not do anything as far as I can recall. The only thing I remember him doing at the house was washing dishes. He said one time that he enjoyed washing dishes, and my rugged outdoorsman of a Dad said 'That man is lying. Ain't no man ever enjoyed washing dishes.' As a result, my Mother-in-law became dependent on me. I picked out a car for her to buy. I also found her a house and negotiated a good deal for her. So she appreciated me quite a bit. She and her husband had two sons. The older one was studious, went to college, then to Seminary. I think he got a Doctorate and became an important official in the Southern Baptist Association. The younger one was the typical rebellious preacher's kid, and they could not control him. But I became a sort of role model for him, and he liked me. I got him interested in football, and he became a pretty good linebacker, I think, because he liked to hit people. He told people I saved his life. After he had grown, he married a very pretty lady. Years afterwards, I ran into him and asked about his wife. He told me they were divorced, and I asked him, "Man, how in the world could you divorce that woman? She was super beautiful." And he replied, "That was the problem. Other men thought she was too!" It was not many years after that that he died at a young age.

Mother-in-law number two was never really close to me, but she liked me. I remodeled her house and did a lot of chores for her and her husband. So they appreciated me, but we never became good friends. I did more for her husband, like bushhogging the field.

Mother-in-law number three was totally different. She liked me from the start. I think her mindset at the time was similar to that of my mother. It really did not matter too much who the new partner was, because they knew that they would like him more than the one who was leaving the family. I recall one Sunday morning at her house, my wife (girlfriend at the time) and I were getting ready to go to church, and I was ironing my shirt. She sat there and watched me for a few minutes, and then she asked, "Charlie, who taught you to iron?" My nickname or alias was Charlie, and all of Carolyn's kinfolk called me that. That did not sit well with my Mother. She would say "I do not have a son named Charlie; his name is Harold!" But I sort of liked Charlie, and it has stuck with that side of the family until this day. Anyway, when she asked, I said, "The United States Air Force and my mother taught me to iron." And she said, "Well, you iron the right way. Carolyn never learned to iron right."

Another time, she had come to visit our new house prior to our wedding, and the two of us were standing in our front yard, admiring the house. She said, "Now, Charlie, if y'all are planning on living together, y'all need to get married. You know it wouldn't be right." I took her advice because that was our plan, but I told her, "No, Ma'am. We don't want to get married. We are going to hang all four divorce certificates above the fireplace with a sign above them that reads 'This is why we are not getting married'. She knew I was joking. She later told me, "Charlie, as far as I am concerned, you are the only son-in-law I have ever had. If you and Carolyn ever decide to get a divorce, you can come live with me." There had been five before me, by the way.

Carolyn never cared for it very much, but Mama liked breakfast, and so did I. We agreed that breakfast was the most important meal of the day. She would enjoy cooking sausage, bacon, grits, eggs, gravy, and – oh me – the best biscuits you ever put in your mouth. Needless to say, she was my favorite. When she got too old to take care of herself, she lived with us for the last two and one-half years of her life.

Chapter Thirty-Seven
Vegas Homes
1982

I told you about losing two prestigious jobs as the Vice President of a Mortgage Company and as the Executive Director of the Housing Program. Eventually, I would end up with a good career, but in the interim, I will tell you this: at times, it was slim-picking and downright embarrassing for me to be out of work while my wife made our living. My first follow-up job was as a representative of a mobile home manufacturing company called Vegas Homes in Yazoo City, Mississippi. Two brothers were the owners, and while they were likeable guys, they were not always the most ethical people in the world. They suggested short-cuts and sometimes questionable, if not downright illegal, methods of moving their product. One of their schemes was to pull a house (trailer) up to a retailer, and as they were trying to convince him to add their line to his inventory, and while making their sales pitch, one of their units was sitting on their lot. Then, while the unit was sitting there, a paid couple would drive up, look around, and fall in love with our unit. Then they would buy it on the spot, pay in cash, hook it up, and drive off. If the sales pitch was successful, the dealer would say, "Man, I got to have some of these. Bring me a dozen. Of course, afterwards the sold unit would be returned to the factory or hauled down the road to the next retailer, and the 'buyers' would be paid for their trouble.

I did not want to get involved in their schemes, so I talked them into letting me set up my own outlet and handle nothing but their homes. This worked out pretty well for about a year, with me operating as a one-man show and contracting for hauling and set-ups. But I had a small lot in a strip mall and could situate only one home on it. Later, I ran into a former friend who had a one-man used auto business and who had a large unused lot, and we went into a partnership. We sold cars on the right side of our building and mobile homes on the left side. Again, we did okay, but we parted ways when my partner let his nephew take one of our trucks off the lot, and he blew the engine. I wanted reimbursement for the truck repair, and my partner wanted to just forget it. It didn't get ugly or turn into a fight; we just mutually decided to part ways while we were still friends. I took my mobile home back to my original, smaller location, and he kept his car dealership. Then two things happened shortly afterwards. First, my landlord suddenly dropped dead of a massive heart attack while he was raking leaves, and secondly, my mobile home supplier disappeared. He came to see me at my place of business one day with an opportunity that I could not refuse. He offered to sell me an $11,000.00 house for $6,500.00 cash. I immediately ran down to the bank, got the money, gave it to him, and took title to the house. After that, I never saw him again. A couple of weeks later, an FBI Agent showed up at my place and started asking me a lot of questions about him. I told him that I had not seen him, nor spoken with him on the phone, for two weeks. After another couple of weeks or so, he called me and told me the story. There was a well-known sports celebrity in Louisiana who was printing counterfeit money, and my mobile home supplier had been transporting it to Florida for laundering. He had been running from the law, but told me he had decided to turn himself in to the authorities. He did and was sentenced to a jail term. So I lost my landlord, the building, and the display lot, and I lost my supplier all within a month. I was out of business and out of a job – again.

Chapter Thirty-Eight
Southern Steel
1984

There was a company in New Orleans, Louisiana called Southern Steel and Aluminum that had a Regional Office in Shreveport, and a Branch Office in Jackson, Mississippi. The Branch Office had been struggling financially for some time, and the remote owners fired its Manager and were going to shut it down. But the Regional Manager persuaded them to let him give it another try, and he ran a local advertisement for a Branch Manager. I applied, went to Shreveport for an interview, and was hired. After a six-week training period in Shreveport, I returned to Jackson and undertook the job of revitalizing the business. It was a wholesale supplier of fencing material with only four employees. I met with them; explained our predicament; and laid out a plan of success. They enthusiasticly signed on, mostly because they wanted to continue to get paid, and we all went to work. First, we gave the place a face-lift by clearing underbrush, repairing and painting the building, building and stocking parts bins and adding a covered loading dock. As Manager, I personally visited every former client we had lost and was successful in reclaiming most of them. We had a good little, close-knit business and started making a profit again. We made a sizable profit the very first year. We received a letter of commendation from the remote owners. It was a lot of fun. The owners let me run the business as if it was my own, without interference or even phone calls. In all my time there, I never met the owners from New Orleans, but they wrote me a letter saying Thank you and said I was a "miracle worker". But the business had a downside as well. We were buying American-made material, and that cost more than the imported stuff. My customers began telling me that my wholesale prices to them were higher than their competitors were charging their retail customers. I finally had to convey this message to the Regional Manager and told him that we had two choices: one, we could start using the lesser quality imported material so we could compete, or two, we would eventually be forced out of business. They decided to stay with American-made products, and our profits dwindled. After eighteen months there, I turned in my resignation and moved to Alabama. The company hired another Manger, but in three months they closed their doors and bulldozed the building. After I moved to Alabama, I opened a business called FENCO - The Fence Company - and began installing fences on the retail level. Our business started slowly, but began growing right away. I hired a few guys to work with me and we did fairly well. We were in business from 1985 to 1989, and our business increased each year.

Chapter Thirty-Nine
Move to Alabama Happy Church
1985

After we moved to Alabama, I got a job with the U.S. Army Corps of Engineers in Mobile. We joined the First Baptist Church of Bay Minette, and I started teaching Sunday School. I am going to tell you something. It felt so good to be back in a Godly environment and to be out from under the demands of an ungodly lifestyle. After six months at FBC, we joined the little country church where I grew up. I continued to teach Sunday School. Actually, I started a new class for people who had suffered a divorce or a rough life, who were not always accepted by the religious crowd, and who wanted a fresh start. In fact, I named our class New Beginnings. I was told that there was no Sunday School room for us, so we met in the Fellowship Hall. The very first Sunday, we had eighteen people in our class at a church where six or seven was the average class size. My wife headed up an organization for women, and hers was the largest women's group. We were both successful and were happy. We stayed there until we moved to Washington, D.C. In 1989.

Chapter Forty
The U.S. Army
1985

One day, when I was in town on business, I stopped by the Employment Office and noticed a job announcement for a Realty Specialist with the U.S. Army Corps of Engineers. Since I had fourteen years of experience in related real estate positions, I decided to apply for it. The Government moves slowly, and after hearing nothing from them, I decided to move back to Jackson and re-enter the mortgage business. But something happened to change my mind. My wife and I had gone to visit her mother in Mississippi and got home around midnight. I told her I was going to retrieve the mail. She said 'Why don't you wait until tomorrow morning', but I told her I wanted it now. Well, in the mail was a card from the Mobile Engineer District inviting me to come in for an interview. Just a few days afterwards, it was followed up with a phone call asking if I were interested. I said I was and went in for an interview, and was hired. The starting salary was lower than I was used to, but at least it was regular, and the job had good benefits. I worked at the Mobile Engineer District, Civil Works Division. With the Civil Works, my duties included inspecting Corps land and recommending our leasing to States, Counties, Cities, or private individuals when our land or facilities were underutilized. I wrote leases, easements, permits, and licenses to authorize the use by others, and then ensured compliance with the instruments. I also inspected our property for violations or encroachments and reported my findings to our legal department. The job was enjoyable as it took me to numerous rivers, lakes, marinas, and public parks. Again, I was industrious and studied hard, which led to a recognition of my dedication. Unbeknownst to me, I was being noticed in Washington, D.C.

Chapter Forty-One
Let's Go to D.C.
1989

After I had been in Mobile for four years, my boss called me into his office and told me that the Army Materiel Command Headquarters (HQAMC) was looking for a Realty Specialist and that he had recommended me for the job. He wasn't sure if it was located in Maryland, Washington D.C., or Virginia, but knew it was close to D.C. It turned out to be in Alexandria, Virginia, just across the Potomac River from Washington, D.C. I was not sure I was ready to make a major move like that, but I agreed to be contacted. Not long afterwards, I got a call from the Chief of the Real Estate Division at HQAMC and was interviewed over the telephone. He said he would be back in touch before long. I hung up and waited. I did not hear anything from him, and soon forgot about the call. Then about three months later, he called again. I told him that I had forgotten all about the job after I never heard from him. He said the Personnel Department should have sent me a letter, but they failed do it. He apologized, and told me that I had been his first choice all along, but that he was forced to hire a black female applicant instead. Then he said that a second opening had become available, and if I wanted the job, it was mine; no further interview was necessary. He also said that he could assure me of a promotion within one year if I kept my nose clean. He told me that I was allotted three travel days for the trip and to report on Monday, December 5th.

Well, the Iron Bowl was on December 3rd, and I did not want to miss that. So I asked if I could delay my arrival by a few days, and he said, "No problem." So I watched Bama beat Auburn that Saturday. Then I left Ms. Duck at home to arrange for the move with the Army-contracted movers, and I headed for Alexandria, Virginia, close to Washington, D.C. I reported for duty on December 7th during a snow storm. In fact, the office closed at noon, so on my very first day at work, I got off half the day. My little television had been damaged on the trip, so I walked across the icy street to a shopping mall and bought another one so I could watch the college football bowls. Then on December 22, 1989, I flew back to Alabama to pick up my wife and drive her back to Virginia. It was six degrees when I left Washington, D.C., and it was nine degrees when I landed in Mobile, Alabama. The Mobile River had frozen over from bank to bank. Man, it was cold! But we made the drive back without any problems and went house hunting. We could not get over the sticker shock in Virginia. In Alabama, we were paying $350 per month for rent; there, the cheapest we could find, clean enough to live in, was a townhouse for about $900. We ended up staying in Virginia for ten years. Before I was offered the job at HQAMC, on two occasions, we had a visitor come to the Mobile Engineer District from Washington, D.C., and he asked if I would be interested in moving to D. C. and working at the Corps of Engineers Headquarters. I turned him down both times, but when the HQAMC job came along, I realized that I would not be promoted at the Mobile Engineer District and decided to make the move.

Chapter Forty-Two
Virginia Churches
1989

When I accepted the job with the U. S. Army Headquarters, and moved to Virginia, we joined a church there and I was voted in as a deacon, even though I had been divorced. That was in Franconia, Virginia. After several years there, we moved to Woodbridge, and I taught Sunday School there. After a year or so, we bought a big, beautiful house in Fredericksburg and moved there in 1995. Again, I immediately started teaching Sunday School. That was our perfect church with a good Pastor and good members. After one year, I was elected as the Chairman of the Deacons (for the third time), and we really enjoyed that church, that community, our new friends, and our new house. We men had a good relationship and performed a lot of jobs around the church. We were notified of a very small church in Pennsylvania that needed help. So seventeen of us guys loaded trucks with tools and drove up there. They had poured a concrete slab on the ground, but had no building. Three days later, we had completely finished a 2400 square foot building. I really liked it there.

Once when my brother and my Dad visited, Dad and I were sitting on our front porch, enjoying the beautiful countryside. He commented, 'Well, boy, I don't guess you will never move back to Alabama, will you?' and I replied, 'You are probably right, Pop. This place feels like my forever home.' Well, it was not to be. In 1997, my mother died, and one day my sister called me crying and said, 'You have to move back to Alabama. I cannot do anything with Daddy, and he is impossible to deal with. You are the only one he will listen to.' My brother, who lived next door to Daddy, had dementia from contact with Agent Orange in Vietnam and was not able to help.

Chapter Forty-Three
The Real Army
1989

The job at HQAMC was completely different from that at the Corps of Engineers. This was the real Army. Our Command was responsible for the manufacturing, maintaining, repairing, and storing everything needed by a Soldier. We were responsible for logistics, having the right equipment in the right place at the right time, and making sure it was in perfect working condition. It was an enormous outfit, with a 4-Star General as its Commander. In fact, I think our Command had about thirty-four General Officers when I arrived and was responsible for something like 172 Army installations and sub-activities. I was responsible for the real estate activities in twenty-two states, which kept me traveling a lot of the time. At the Corps, almost all the employees were civilians, with the exception of our Commander, who was an Army Colonel, and maybe a couple of Staffers. The AMC Headquarters had a lot of civilian workers too, but there we were treated as Active Military officers, with comparable duties and ranks. Being located in or near Washington, D. C. also meant it operated in a very competitive and aggressive environment. I was at a disadvantage because I was a 'red-neck' from south Alabama and because I was a Christian. I was shunned by the Commander at meetings several times and received a few awards in secret behind the scenes and unknown to my co-workers. Once, while he was handing out awards, his secretary said. "You forgot this one for Harold, and he told her, 'I am saving it for later. When 'later' came next month, he walked past my desk and laid it on my table without ever announcing it and said rather softly, 'These people want you to know that they think you are doing a good job'. Then he raved to the group about a black female excelling in physical fitness. That is how it was during his entire assignment there, but thank goodness it finally ended, and we got a very nice and decent Colonel in his place. And we had one 4-Star General Commander whom I really liked. He was a black man from Louisiana, and although he wore four stars on his shoulders and was the top official in the organization, he never acted superior to us workers. He used to stop by my desk just for a chat every week or two. I really liked him. And again, I studied hard and took advantage of every training exercise available to me. As a result, I received many commendations and awards. I was chosen to be on the team that rewrote four Army Regulations; I was chosen to be an Instructor for the Army Real Estate school and taught real estate classes to all our installations. I rotated between Baltimore, Huntsville, Rock Island, and Seattle. And I applied for the Army Management Staff College, the equivalent of the secular Graduate School, and was accepted. More on that in the next chapter.

Chapter Forty-Four
U.S. Army Staff College
1994

As a student at the Army Management Staff College, I wrote numerous papers and made many speeches. I stayed up until 1:00 a.m. many nights studying and writing. My dissertation, which I wrote for the Army Management Staff College (equivalent to a civilian college thesis), was selected for induction into the Fort Belvoir library as a learning tool for future students. I made a grade of A+ on every written assignment and only one 95 on an oral assignment when I went over the allotted time. Way to go – Motor-mouth! All the people who know me will laugh at this; I like to talk. I was successful and was promoted quickly. When I started with the Corps, I was a GS-09, and at the end of four years, I was a GS-11, one promotion. I was hired at HQ, AMC as a GS-12, and one year and eleven months later, I was a GS-14, which was equal to a Lt. Colonel, and which set a record for rapid advancement. We interacted with active Military Officers every day and were always respected and treated as equals. I spent a lot of time in the Pentagon, and actually lost a friend and colleague in the attack on September 11, 2001. A GS-14 was equivalent to a Lieutenant-Colonel, but just prior to my departure from the Headquarters, I was awarded the rank of Colonel, although I never really earned that rank. But it was a recognition I cherished, and I have a copy of my Geneva Convention card that reads "06/COL" framed and hanging on my office wall to this day.

Chapter Forty-Five
The Gulf War
1990

I had been at AMC for less than one year when I was deployed to Saudi Arabia in support of Operation Desert Shield/Desert Storm; the war with Iraq. Duty in a battle zone was hard, working twelve hours a day, first seven days a week, and then reduced to six. But even though it was demanding and tiring, it was also rewarding because we were supporting the fighting soldiers, and it was easy to see that it was a worthwhile effort. I was not there very long, only seven weeks. The Field Commander there has sent an urgent request to our Headquarters saying he needed a Real Estate engineer on site immediately, and I was sent to fill that immediate need until we could find a permanent person to take my place. But I almost ended up in the Brig in Saudi Arabia. The war against Iraq was an International Joint venture, and several countries deployed soldiers there to assist the United States. I met soldiers from the United Kingdom, Jamaica, and I think there were some from France, Italy, and Spain, although I am not certain of that. Japan, however, did not send any soldiers; its national law prohibited the deployment of soldiers outside its boundaries. So instead, to show their support and participation, Japan provided us with a fleet of new cars, mostly Toyota's. One day, I was one of a group of people who went to the seaport at Dhahran to pick up a shipment of cars and drive them to the base. While on the way back, we took a short-cut which caused us to drive the wrong way on a one-way street. One of the local policemen fell in behind me, turned on his lights, and tried to pull me over. I ignored him and kept driving, with him behind me the whole time. When I reached the compound, the large parking lot was full, and I had to drive to the backside to find a parking place, while being followed by a policeman. I don't recall a siren, but there may have been one. When I finally parked and got out of the car, he was in my face, obviously perturbed. He tried to put me in his car, but I refused, and after a brief confrontation, I finally gave him my military ID, and he left. I went inside and told the First-Sergeant what had happened, and he told me not to worry about it. After two days, he took me to the Saudi jail where he explained to the Captain what had happened. The Captain said it was a major offense. If one of his troops had done that (driven the wrong way), he would have killed him. At the time, my I. D. card showed I had the rank of a Major, and the jail Captain said, "Oh, Major! You are the boss." I said, "I am, and don't you forget it!" Then he apologized and let me go. By the way, prisoners were not taken care of very well there. A prisoner had to rely on outside family or friends for daily food. We used to joke about being imprisoned for 'Thirty days or life, whichever came first'. Thank goodness, I did not have any further run-ins with the law while stationed there.

I had it pretty good. When I first arrived, I was housed in an eight-foot by twelve-foot plywood room with bunk beds against each wall, with a desk and a clothes locker between. When the Colonel, our Commanding Officer, found out I was there, he told his First Sergeant to move me into the three-bedroom house with them. One day, he asked me, "Duck, why is it that all the other Officers here are driving Mercedes and I have a Toyota?" I replied, "I will get you a Mercedes, Sir. So the next night I left the Toyota headlights on, and the next morning it failed to crank. The Motor Pool said the battery was dead, and replaced it with a new one. I did the same thing that night, and sure enough, the Toyota did not start the next morning. I went to the Motor Pool and told them that my Commanding Officer was fed up with that car, and I did not want a new battery; I wanted a new Mercedes. Then I drove up to the Colonel and asked, "How do you like your new car, Sir?" He laughed and said "Duck, you are a miracle-worker. I knew I wanted you on my team." From that day on, I chauffered the Colonel around in a new Mercedes.

Now I want to tell you an amusing story. I cannot vouch for its accuracy one-hundred percent, but I do know parts of it to be truthful. I told you our mission at the Headquarters was to have the right equipment at the right place at the right time and to ensure it was in proper working order. Well, I don't think we accomplished that mission when the war first started. First, some of our equipment was not in working order. Then we had to change the color from Jungle Green in Vietnam to Sandy Beige in Saudi Arabia. Some was late getting there. Later on, after the war had ended, we were told in a security briefing that if Iraq had started a couple of weeks earlier, we may not have won. But here is the funny part. Dan Rather was reporting on the war from the roof of our Administration Building and he would report on the equipent as it arrived. I was told that a huge C-5A aircraft would come in, land and unload five tanks. The tanks would be loaded on a flat-bed truck and leave. Not too long afterwards another plane load of tanks would appear and would be unloaded. Now here is what I was told that I cannot validate, but have no reason to doubt. After the tanks were loaded on the flat-bed truck, they would be taken to the far side on the base, and be loaded on the C-5A plane. Then they would be transported to the front of the base where Dan Rather was reporting about the massive number of tanks we were bringing there. Same plane; same tanks. Military propaganda. But it worked, because Iraq was keeping an eye on it.

During the early stage of the war, our 4-Star General disappeared with no explanation for about a month or two, and later returned and laughed 'Well, I am back. Turned out he was being grilled by the Pentagon.

Chapter Forty-Six
The EOC
1991

After my return to the Headquarters from Saudi Arabia, I was the Real Estate Point of Contact in the Emergency Operation Center for Desert Storm, a position I held until the end of the war. My job was to receive daily status reports from the field and then brief the General and other top staffers on the activities. As a result, I received several citations from the General Officers. After the war, I resumed my regular duties as a Realty Specialist responsible for the management of installations assigned to me. One of my duties was to draft replies for the Congressmen or Congresswomen who had received letters from his/her constituents that concerned one of my installations. One day, I was handed a letter from a Congress men who had received a complaint from a private individual about a soldier speeding through the Louisiana Army Ammunition Plant, and was told to draft a letter as the Congressman's response to this private individual. My letter had to pass through the Congressional Liaison Office at our Headquarters for approval or editing, so I carried it up to their office. On my first visit to the Congressional Liaison Officer, I was overwhelmed. I met a beautiful lady, and she had Crimson Tide paraphernalia all over her walls and desk.

I felt right at home. We talked Bama football for a long time, and from then on, I did not have any trouble having my Congressional inquiry letters approved. Even with the stress that came with the job, I enjoyed my stay in the D. C. area. It was a rewarding job and one that made me feel I was doing something worthwhile. We also liked Virginia a lot and visited every area of the state.

146

Chapter Forty-Seven
Alabama Again
1999

In 1995, we moved from Alexandria to Fredericksburg, Virginia, and bought a brand new, very nice two-story home under construction that was situated on a three-acre lot; something that was impossible to get in Alexandria. We loved the house and the new subdivision and were happy campers. In May 1996, Dwight and Dad came for a visit, and one afternoon as Dad and I were sitting on the front porch admiring the surroundings, he commented to me, "Well, Boy, I guess you won't ever move back to Alabama, will you?" And I replied, "No, Sir, I don't think I will.

But that would not be the case. In 1997, my Mother died following a heart attack. I flew to Mobile to be with her in the hospital for her last days on earth and then to attend her funeral. Then in 1998, I got a call from my Sister who told me that my Dad's health was failing, both physically and mentally, and asked me if I could move back to Alabama to help take care of him. My brother lived close to Dad, but he was unable to do anything because he was suffering from dementia. He got exposed to Agent Orange in Vietnam and subsequently died at age 62.

So I applied for a 'Compassionate Reassignment' with the Army, but was denied because AMC and the COE were two different Major Commands. But I found a person at the Mobile Engineer District who was interested in moving to D. C. and began the task of a job-swap program. It took seventeen months, but we finally pulled it off, and in 1999, I once again became an employee of the Mobile Alabama District Corps of Engineers. This time, I was assigned to the Military Branch rather than the Civil Branch. My primary job was the disposition of land and facilities belonging to the Army and the Air Force that had been declared excess under the Base Closure and Realignment Program (known as BRAC), a position I had held in D.C. I was named as the Transfer Agent for the Government for the transfer of the real property to prospective owners or purchasers. I had free rein of the program, partly because my supervisor did not know much about the BRAC process and partly because I outranked him, and he didn't know what to do with me. At the start of BRAC, under the Clinton Administration, if a city, county, or state could show a plan of proposed development that would result in a significant creation of new jobs, they could qualify for what was known as an Economic Development Transfer, which would enable them to receive a deed to the property and improvements at no cost. Most times, the plan would cover a period of fifteen years, which I monitored at given intervals. I met with a lot of Mayors and city officials to explain the program and assist them in their application. I also became friends with a few Congressmen, especially Congressman Bob Riley, who later became Governor of the State of Alabama. I was the key-note speaker at one transfer ceremony where Congressman Riley was on the program. It was an enjoyable job, and when the excess Government property was transferred, I was a local hero.

Then, after President Bush became president, the Government changed its policy and required an appraisal and the payment of a fair price. So I became the Lead Negotiator for the sale of excess government property for the Army and the Air Force. My biggest achievement was selling 15 waterfront acres that the Air Force had used as an officer housing site for $3.4 Million. I still have the Certificate of Appreciation and a copy of the check. I stayed with the Corps until the BRAC program played itself out, and then was appointed Chief of the Civil Works Branch. But I did not like being the boss, and after six months, I decided to call it quits and retire.

Chapter Forty-Eight
Here We Are Again
1999

We moved back to Alabama primarily to take care of my old Dad. But that job fell to my wife while I was at work with the U.S. Army Corps of Engineers in Mobile. Believe me, hers was not an easy task. She called me more than once, crying, 'That's the meanest man I have ever met.' I met her at the cemetery one day, and as we sat on Mother's headstone, I recalled her telling me while she was on her deathbed, 'Y'all are really going to have a hard time taking care of your Daddy after I am gone." She could not have been more correct. It was a constant job. He would put a bowl of grits in the microwave and turn it to the highest setting, flinging grits everywhere. He would pour a cup of coffee and dribble it on the floor to the back door. She cleaned the little house out back that he lived in, and got chewed out and told to never do that again. He had it just like he wanted it. There was more, but I will not labor the point here. Anyway, Carolyn sacrificed her freedom and her sanity to take care of him for three years until Daddy went to a Nursing Home in 2002.

Chapter Forty-Nine
Church Confusion
2000

I told you about my early start in church attendance. As a child, church never really bothered me; in fact, I enjoyed it. However, as I matured, I came to realize that the church had various facets. After I figured out that God was not calling me to preach, I started paying attention to the secular or administrative side of the church. I have had many pleasant experiences in church and some very disappointing ones as well. Over the years, I have held various positions of leadership in a number of churches. I served as a Deacon in four different churches. I have taught numerous study courses in more than one church. I taught Sunday School for approximately twenty years. I quickly grew tired of printed, prepared lessons and began studying the Bible and writing my own lessons. I am still doing that at this writing. Along with my wife, Carolyn, we undertook numerous church projects, including landscaping, floral arrangements, home dinners for church friends, church-wide backyard cookouts, and more. However, I learned that church, of all places, is one of the easiest places to get into disagreements. I think many of the disagreements are based on power struggles, politics, and aggressive ambition. Too many people want to be front and center, or to be the preacher's pets, or to be considered the church hero. Too many times, church leadership or participation does not lend itself to humility, but promotes and encourages jealousy and pride. And you know what the Bible says about pride.

Chapter Fifty
The Little Country Church
2000

Shortly after our move to Alabama, we rejoined that little country church where we had been before, and resumed our duties and positions we had before.

But then the devil raised his head and started causing problems. Some members became jealous and started making unkind remarks against us. They openly accused me of trying to take over the church and accused my wife of disrupting the WMU. One woman in particular was the main trouble maker. She claimed her grandfather founded that church, and as far as she was concerned, it was hers to run. She got the preacher on her side. I went to talk to him about her and here is what he said to me; 'Listen, that lady and her husband give far more money to this church than any other family, and I am not about to do anything that will cause flack with her.' So much for fairness and justice. Then I did something that made him mad at me. This woman had paid $32,000 for the steeple on the church as a tribute and monument to her husband, and she had a dedication service where she announced it to the church and called for special recognition and appreciation. This did not sit well with me, and since I was the Chairman of the Memorial Committee, I called a meeting without informing the pastor and passed a vote to prohibit such action to any living person. This made the pastor furious at me. Then I learned that this preacher had his name engraved on a plaque at his former church. That set the stage and made me the enemy, and he never let it go.

I had become tired and discouraged. This controlling woman was really controlling my time and my mind. She claimed her grand-father donated the land and built the church in 1910, and was quick to point out that the church bore his name. But when I went to the courthouse and looked up the deed records, I found out that was not the case. And it really bothered me that no one had the guts to stand up to her. So I realized it was time for me to leave, but it was still a difficult thing to do. But I did not leave right away. I let things rock on, and the preacher and I sort of kept our distance. I resigned from all committees and as a Deacon and enjoyed teaching Sunday School, and doing a number of construction projects at the Church.

Chapter Fifty-One
Get Rid of Harold
2012

Well, that little episode with the Memorable Committee was not enough to get me kicked out of his church, but the preacher never let go of his anger. He enlisted the help of the deacon chairman, and together they concocted another two-fold story; one involving the church and the other involving my neighbors. Let's do the neighbors first.

Part One - When we bought Dad's old house, we put our house up for sale. A couple decided they wanted it and paid our price. She was a very nice lady, and we became close friends. They invited us up to their mountain home in Pigeon Forge, and we spent New Year's Eve there. New Year's Eve was the biggest broadcast of college bowl games, and I was looking forward to watching them. But our host was not interested in football, and we spent the entire night watching a documentary on World War II. I was disappointed beyond words, but I tolerated it. After all, it was his house.

His wife and my wife became close friends and spent a lot of time together, shopping and going out to eat. I had another lot across from their house, and I decided to sell it too. I asked them if they wanted it, but they did not want to pay my price, so I advertised it in the newspaper. This was six years after they had bought our house, and our visit to their home. When I advertised it, I included a sentence that said 'Mobile homes allowed.' Well, that lady hit the ceiling; I mean, super irate. She cussed me out for saying 'Mobile Homes Welcomed'. She visited three neighbors and talked them into joining her fight against me, one of whom told me on two occasions 'You are my best friend on earth'. All three were living on land that I had sold to them. They all liked me when they bought my land. But this lady, who was such a close friend, called my wife and said she was coming to get me. My wife told her that I was leaving for a deacon's meeting, so she proceeded to cuss her out as well – her best friend. Then she called the preacher during the deacon's meeting, and he excused himself from the meeting and stayed on the phone a long time, eating up everything she said. She accused me of breaking and entering, stealing, and lying.

Chapter Fifty-Two
Church Accusations
2012

After getting an earful from my neighbor, the preacher called the chairman of the deacons and told him how bad I was. But that is not all. They also brought in a report concerning my behavior in church.

Part Two – The two of them (preacher and deacon) said that six women had approached them out of the blue and had accused me of inappropriate sexual behavior in church. I asked who the six women were, and they told me. So I said, 'Okay, we will call these six women up front during a Sunday morning service and let them tell the church. Then the church can decide what to do with me'. They replied, 'Oh no! We are not going to reveal their names to the church.' So I contacted all six of these women – or at least I attempted to. They were all well-known to me and were personal friends. We hugged at church, but no 'inappropriate sexual behavior'. Four of the six immediately denied this: they said that they had never complained about me, and one said, 'I don't even know Mister Deacon; why would I say anything to him?' The two that did not deny the charges were the wife of the preacher and the wife of the deacon. Now ain't that surprising! Go figure! When I could not reach them by phone, I sent an email. The preacher's wife replied 'Well, I have always felt that your hugs were inappropriate'. But she had hugged me – and many other men in the church - for six years without complaining. Ms. Deacon's wife would not answer my calls and would not respond to my email. But one day, my wife ran into her and her husband in the grocery store, and she called out to her, but she ignored her. So my wife got closer and made her talk. At this point, her husband just walked away. Then, when my wife asked why she said that about me, she said, 'I have just always felt uneasy when I was around your husband.' Now, this couple was two of our best friends; we visited and ate at each other's house; we went to the Beau Rivage together to see Lord of the Rings; we rode together to New Orleans to attend a marriage counseling session; we went to Pensacola for a Valentine's supper; he and I did numerous construction jobs at the church. I mean, we were as close as two friends have ever been. But his pastor convinced him to join the fight against me. The preacher called him and told him 'It's bad; it's really bad'. We have got to have a meeting with him. So on Thursday, the deacon called me and asked me to meet with them on Saturday to face the charges – not to defend myself; the jury had already reached a verdict. After hearing all the untruthful lies and charges, I got mad and threw my church keys across the table and stormed out. It almost got into a fist fight. I understood that I was no longer welcome there, in my home church, and these two guys were both outsiders. I want to tell you that the episode really tore me up, along with my wife, mentally, spiritually, and physically. But thanks to God, he brought us through it and put us in a better place.

I met with my Sunday School class the next day and told them what happened. Every one of them quit Sunday school with the exception of the woman who wanted to be the teacher, her husband and her grand-daughter, and one of the deacons who was sympathic to the preacher. So the largest SS class in the church fizzled out to nothing (maybe four people) immediately. [There is a lot more to this story that I have not included here.]

Chapter Fifty-Three
Back to Part One
2012

Now to finish Part One – about the neighbors - of course, that lady and I stopped being close friends, but I never did act ugly toward her, even though she accused me of bad behavior, including theft of property, breaking and entering, and aggressive actions. One day I was working out in my back yard and her little dog ran up to me. So I picked him up and soon afterwards this lady came walking up, said Thank You, took the dog, and started to walk off. Then she turned around and said, 'I owe you an apology,' and I said, 'For what?' She said I got so mad at you for saying mobile homes were allowed on your lot you had for sale, that I went to our neighbors and talked them into making up charges and accusations against you. None of them were true; I made it all up'. And I said, 'Don't worry about it; it upset me a lot when it was happening, but now I am over it, and it really worked out for the best.' We did not hug or shake hands, but we have been friends ever since.

I contacted that preacher and told him what she said, and asked him to enter a note in the church business meeting minutes that all the charges against me were untrue and that my name had been cleared. He refused. I want to tell you something, my friend, it took me a very long time to forgive those two church officials. Since then, I have offered a reconciliation, but it has been refused each time. So I left that church. Today, both of those wives, along with my wife, have died.

Man – what an ordeal – and from all these 'Christian' people.

Chapter Fifty-Four
The Church of Rest
2012

During my adult life, I have been a member or an attendee of probably 15 or 20 churches, mostly due to my physical relocation. After we left Virginia, we became members of a small church in our community, and I would like to share the story of how we got there. We were members of the little country church where I grew up. I told you earlier about the lady who asserted herself as the controller of the church. Well, when I continued my vocal objection to that situation to the pastor and leadership, they decided their church would be easier if I were not a member there. That is when this eruption took place.

We had no idea where to go to find another church. We visited a couple of places, but did not feel comfortable. We were much too old for a contemporary style, and there were not that many traditional churches to choose from. One day, not long afterwards, we were at the office of our chiropractor, and as we left the parking lot, we noticed a sign in front of a little church that read "Old Fashioned Preaching. I had never noticed the church building until that day, although we had passed it many times. But when I saw the sign, I told my wife, "That's where we are going on Sunday." We did go there, entering with still broken hearts and spirits from the recent events at our former church. That day, the preacher used Matthew Chapter 2 Verses 28 – 30 as his text, and we had no doubt that it was a message from God meant specifically for us. Look at what it says: v.28: "Come unto me, all ye that labour and are heavy laden, and I will give you rest. v.29: "Take my yoke upon you, and learn of me; for I am meek and lowly in heart: and ye shall find rest unto your souls. 30 For my yoke is easy, and my burden is light".

We both left there with tears in our eyes, thanking God for His love and care. After visiting for a while, we joined and stayed there for six years. Now, this church was not perfect; none are, you know, but it had such a sweet and loving spirit among its members that made up for any concerns we may have had. We were greeted with handshakes and hugs that first day we visited, and we have cultivated some very close relationships since that day. It is amazing how God works things out for us if we only trust Him and remain patient, which is sometimes hard to do for me.

That was in 2012. While I agreed with their theology, the preacher acted more like the leader of a cult. He did everything. He led the singing; he taught Sunday School; he did all the preaching; he decided how the money was spent without accountability; he decided which missionaries we were going to support, and how much money we would donate to their cause; he publicly outlawed pants for women, and criticized those with short hair; he decided if flowers could be placed in the sanctuary. He had his hand in everything that happened, and he made every decision and controlled every action that the church took. I asked him if I could teach Sunday School, but he told me that he had that covered. So I did not have to do anything in this church. I was not a deacon or a teacher. I was on a couple of committees, but they did not amount to much of anything. And I turned down the invitation to be a Trustee three times. The Pastor was my friend, and we had several sincere man-to-man talks about all of this, but neither of us changed our thinking. So I told him we were leaving, and we shook hands and parted. We left there in 2018. We are still friends to this day, and I understand he has loosened his grip on most things. In fact, he and another preacher conducted my wife's funeral when she died in October 2024.

Chapter Fifty-Five
Home for Sale
2015

I have probably lived in forty houses since I left my parent's home, and I certainly will not bore you by listing them all here. They included the states of Alabama, Mississippi, Texas, South Carolina, Massachusetts, New Hampshire, and Virginia. I think that the last fifteen have been shared with Carolyn. We have lived in everything from a single-wide mobile home to a few very nice houses. I have already told you about our first home and the one we had in Virginia. But now I want to tell you about one more. My Dad built the house I told you about earlier in 1946. Mother died in 1997. Dad died in 2005. He did not live in the house; he had built himself a small 'man' cabin out back, and the big house sat empty for eight years, during which time it suffered termite and water damage. Dad's last two and one-half years were spent in a nursing home, and Medicaid placed a lien on his house. So when he died, we had to decide what we wanted to do with it. The lien was $111,000.00, and none of my siblings wanted to take it on, so I had them sign over the house to me. Then I negotiated with Medicaid and paid off the lien. I then undertook the task of repairing and rebuilding the old house. I completely gutted it and made everything new. I installed insulation, central air and heat, put on a new roof, rewired and replumbed it, put in new walls, floors, doors, windows, and ceilings. Then I doubled the size. It took me a year and a half to finish it, and it cost me close to $200,000. Then Carolyn put her decorating skills to work and made it look like a bed-and-breakfast. We maintained it in pristine condition. It was actually nominated to

Southern Living and to Better Homes and Gardens as a feature house. Neither of them selected it, but to be nominated was an honor. It was a hard job to keep it looking good, but we maintained it in pristine condition. There was always something that needed to be done, like painting, power washing, raking, and burning leaves, etc. Many a day after we had worked ourselves half to death, we would sit in one of the six swings and comment on how good it looked. Then we would start it all over the next morning. It was surrounded by trees and was home to a lot of birds and squirrels, with an occasional deer, raccoon, opossum, fox, and several armadillos. We added flowerbeds, fountains, swings, benches, fish ponds, and porches and patios. We hosted several Bar-B-Que cookouts for friends and church members who raved over our place. But after nine years, it got too much for us to keep up, and we decided to sell it and move to a smaller place that did not require as much upkeep.

Chapter Fifty-Six
Leave the Country
2016

Now I want to tell you about our current residence and how we got here because we have no doubt that God worked it out for us. At first, we listed the old house For Sale by Owner and got immediate responses. But most people who wanted it could not afford it or failed to qualify for financing, and one by one, all possible sales fell through. A couple of them were outright scams, offering to pay the asking price in cash from Africa and Russia. We learned not to get excited about the offers. We had couples who left in tears because they could not work out a deal. We tried listing it with a Realtor who assured us that it would sell quickly, but here again, all prospects failed to end up in a sale. So we prayed about it and told God 'You know our situation; we are old and tired; and we need to sell this place. We are going to list it one more time, and if it does not work out this time, we will take it as your indication that you want us to stay here until we die'.

This time, we listed it on Zillow as For Sale by Owner, and within two days, we got two calls on it. On day three, we were in the carport giving our big old outside dog a bath when Carolyn's phone rang. Before she answered it, she told me 'That's somebody wanting to see the house'. I said, 'How in the world would you know that? You haven't even answered your phone yet.' Listen, all you husbands, she could have said, 'Because I am a woman, and women know these things. She always knew 'these kinds of things' when I didn't have a clue. She answered the call, and I heard her say 'Well, can you give us thirty minutes? We are bathing our dog now, and will need to change clothes. Okay, we will see you then." Then she said to me, "They are coming to see the house." I did not say a word! Didn't need to!

Now, listen to this story. This is where God took over. It is a two-phased story, but I think you will enjoy it. Phase I - The callers showed up in thirty minutes. They were a young couple, probably in their late twenties, with three little children. From the time they walked in, tears filled her eyes, and she said 'I have to tell you a story. For months and months, we have been looking for a house. We are currently living in a small house close to the University of South Alabama in Mobile, which I bought when I was single. We all sleep in one room. We wanted a big, sprawling, three or four-bedroom house in the country with plenty of space and with a big yard for the kids and dogs to play in. We have seen several, but none of them had all we wanted. This morning, I was praying and asking God to lead us to a place that would fit our needs. Within ten minutes after I had prayed, my husband called and said, 'I have found our house; it just popped up on my cell phone'. So, of course, we got over here as fast as we could. We drove by it yesterday and then came back today. That's why I called you now; we are certain that God found this house for us. It is a perfect place for us, and is exactly what we have been looking for.' We just hugged her neck and told her, 'Welcome to your new home.' Both of them bragged on every room they saw, and her two little girls started squealing, 'This is my room!' It was truly a blessing to see. They wanted it as soon as they could close the deal. They were already pre-approved and had a Realtor lined up, so they called her and scheduled a closing. We were extremely happy, but it created a dilemma for us. We had looked around a bit, but had not decided on any house, and now we needed to get out as soon as possible.

Chapter Fifty-Seven
Home for Us
2016

Now here is Phase II – We hit the road that very afternoon, canvassing neighborhoods we liked. We spent all the next day with a Real Estate agent and saw many houses, but most did not offer everything on our wish-list, and the ones that did were too expensive. We did ride by one in a development that looked okay and wrote down the number on the For Sale Sign, but never seriously considered it. Then we went further south and started talking to a builder who had several houses under construction. We got pretty serious about one that was about two months from completion, but we knew we needed something sooner. Finally, partly out of desperation, we decided to call the number we had noted earlier and asked the Realtor if she had time to meet us in the late afternoon. She agreed, and we met around four or five o'clock that afternoon. God had already helped our buyers; now, here is where He helped us out. We liked the neighborhood; we liked the level, corner lot; we liked the side-loading garage; we liked the exterior of the house. Then we walked inside and were flabbergasted. Our wish list contained an open plan - this house had it; a formal dining room - this house had it; a large office - this house had it; a split bedroom plan - this house had it; a large master bedroom, and a large master bath with a tub and a walk-in shower, plus a walk-in closet - this house had it; a sunroom - this house had it; and a screened porch - this house had it, and with an outdoor fireplace. Trouble is, it was $10,000 over our budget. So right there on the spot, we made an offer for $10,000 less than the asking price. I think it was two days, maybe three, that the real estate lady called to say our offer had been accepted. Plus, the seller left us some furniture, a television, and some tools and lumber. Believe me, we thanked God right there and started packing. We did everything in a matter of two weeks. Who says that God does not notice what is going on and doesn't help those who trust Him? What a wonderful and direct blessing, and to this day, we are still thankful for His help. We lived there for eight years, and met some nice neighbors; have added some improvements; and Carolyn has put her finishing decorating touches on the interior. That is not quite true – I don't think she ever gets completely through. But she has fun, and that is what is important. Hey, I just enjoy mowing for twenty minutes rather than for four hours, and for having no leaves to rake or wooden structures to repair. Every day I look around and say 'I like it here;. And then I say, 'Thank you, God.' We are now close to our church, our drug store, our pharmacy, doctors, shopping, and Lowe's! Life is good.

Actually, we looked at another house later on that we liked, which is an interesting story, but I am saving that for the last chapter.

Chapter Fifty-Eight
The Intermission
2018

After we left what I called 'The Church of Rest', where we had no jobs or positions, we visited a few other churches. Some were contemporary and modern, which were too much for my old age. Then we visited First Baptist of Spanish Fort, and we liked it a lot. But we were sort of gun-shy, and we attended as visitors for eleven months before we joined. After joining, we got actively involved and were extremely happy. At first, I thought, how is it possible that we thought that God had led us to the small church and then, after six years, impressed upon us that it was time to move on. But now, looking back on it, it makes perfect sense. You see, when we were at the little country church where I grew up, we were active in everything. I was a Deacon; I taught Sunday School; I was the Director of the men's organization; I was on numerous committees; I did many carpenter and construction projects; you name it – I did it. Carolyn was just as active. She was the Chairperson of the Fellowship Committee, which meant she was in charge of all the church-wide meals and activities. She did all the floral arrangements and landscaping. She was also the leader of the women's organization, which had about thirty members. In short, we were working ourselves to death and were pretty burned out. Then came the six-year period where we did nothing to speak of. We would have, but we were not allowed to. We were forced to rest, whether we wanted to or not. I don't know if we fully understood it at the time, but looking back on it, it is easy to see how God took care of us and worked it all out for our good at His timing. Remember Romans 8:28?

Chapter Fifty-Nine
The First Baptist Church
2018

The First Baptist Church was without a Pastor at the time we started visiting. They had an Interim Pastor filling in, who was a super nice person, and we made friends rather quickly. But because of the trauma of past churches, we were in no hurry to join. The church hired a new pastor in June 2019. Because of a lot of urging by friends, we decided to join in September. The new preacher bought a house in our subdivision and started visiting a lot. He and his wife hit it off pretty well with my wife, and she served them and their daughter numerous meals at our house. Church was pretty good back then, but then dozens of newcomers from another church joined our church and immediately started taking over. Even as this became obvious, the preacher did not have the courage to stand up to them. As a result, there were political decisions and secret back-room meetings, and decisions pushed through. Of course, I voiced my objections to him, but to no avail. The newcomers only grew stronger in number and control.

Chapter Sixty
No Divorce in Our Church
2023

An issue of contention arose concerning divorce. These power guys had written a new set of By-Laws for the church, and had inserted a clause that said the church had earlier voted to ban divorced men as deacons. I checked, and no such vote was ever taken. So I pushed the issue and made a motion that it needed to be decided before the document was voted on. This caused the big shots to become extremely angry, and I became their number one enemy. The pastor went along with them, and I spoke openly against this obvious attempt to make a decision for the church. This finally resulted in my being summoned to a meeting of a few deacons and the pastor, where they stripped me of all participation in the church, including teaching Sunday School. In fact, a few of the deacons were assigned the task of calling all the members of our Sunday School class while the meeting was underway to tell them that I was no longer their teacher. They threatened to have me arrested, handcuffed, and escorted out of the building if I showed up the following Sunday. I have been called a troublemaker, an agitator, an instigator, a stirrer of the pot, among some other things. One man even told the entire congregation that I was 'an agent of Satan'. And in a way, I think they may be right, except for the agent of Satan comment. I have a tendency to speak up when things are being handled the wrong way, and I am not afraid of the consequences.

So once again, my Sunday School class disintegrated and almost disappeared. This happened in May 2024. Again, we were excommunicated from a church that professed to be a loving and kind group. But you need to understand that this was not the attitude of the whole church; it was just the position of these few men who set themselves up as the rulers of the church. The majority of the members were too afraid of these self-appointed rulers to confront them. And of course, they were successful in getting rid of me - their number one trouble maker. The meeting was very disturbing to my wife, causing extreme stress and health problems. Their vicious and cruel attack on me really upset her; she was completely devastated by witnessing firsthand how mean, brutal, and inhumane a church group could be. She was already in bad health, and with this extreme additional stress, she did not survive. She died in October of that year, due to a large part as a result of this meeting. So we were out of church. I instructed the church secretary to remove my name from the roll and from all records of my ever having been a member there. But several members of my Sunday School class asked me to start conducting Sunday School classes in my home, which I did until the death of my wife.

Chapter Sixty-One
Friends
2025

I learned the hard way that a church and church people can be the cruelest people on earth. I find it very hard to trust people who profess to be super Christians anymore. Thank God He has blessed me with a small group of close and trust-worthy friends who have been a tremendous help to me as I went through all these disasters. I recently found a very small church that I have attended for several Sundays now. The Pastor is the very same man who was the Interim Pastor of the First Baptist Church when we first started visiting there. It was a real pleasure to connect with him again. I enjoy going there, but I have no idea if I will ever become a member. Odds are that I probably will not. For some strange reason, I am not really keen on joining another church. Time and God will decide.

Chapter Sixty-Two
My Bout with Covid-19
2021

I realize that this story is out of order chronologically, but it really did not fit, so I am putting it here. At the age of seventy-eight, I contracted the very worst case of Covid-19, along with double pneumonia. This is my account of that horrible ordeal. It is a weird story with two very different and separate versions, both of which are very real, at least in my mind. It started on Wednesday night, July 14, 2021, when I went to the mid-week service at our church. At the time, I did not know that anything was wrong, but the congregation was being exposed to the Covid virus, and I was one of about thirty people who contracted it. By Friday, I was coughing constantly, nonstop, and could hardly breathe.

On Saturday, I mowed the lawn, which only made it worse. Of course, Carolyn tried to convince me to go to the doctor, but I passed it off as a sinus infection and did not go. Sunday was even worse, and on Monday, I knew I had a serious condition and agreed to let her take me to the Urgent Care Center in Malbis. When I got there, my oxygen level was dangerously low, and they wanted to call an ambulance to take me to the Thomas Hospital Emergency room. Instead, Carolyn drove me there, and I sat in the ER with an oxygen tank hooked up to me for an unknown period of time. I do not know if I passed out or if they put me to sleep, but I have no recollection of anything after that for the next three or four weeks. I was told that they put me in the ICU and put a ventilator in my mouth and throat. Now this is where it gets weird.

Chapter Sixty-Three
Unconscious Trips

In my unconscious state, I was one hundred percent sure that Thomas Hospital sent me to the Mobile Infirmary, where I was examined by a team of doctors. When they were unsure of how to treat me, they transferred me to Forest General Hospital in Hattiesburg, Mississippi, with the same outcome. But I was not admitted at first. Somehow, I was put on a little bus and was moved to a small room full of ladies at William Carey University, where I had attended college. I remember all those women chattering away and how irritated I became with them. But I was unable to talk. Finally, they quieted down for the night, and I was left separated in a corner of the room, lying on an army cot. I had some sort of bag attached to my arm, which inflated and deflated regularly. Occasionally, one of the staff members would come over and peer at me, look puzzled at my arm bag, shake her head, and walk away. Later, she would return. This happened about four times, and then she brought another lady with her. They decided to send me to a remote care facility outside the city limits of Hattiesburg. There, they stripped me naked and gave me a bath. Not a normal bath; they put me on a table and washed me down with a garden hose. A guy named Charlie gave me the bath, and he was downright sadistic with aggressive force, being extra rough in the body parts where he should have been extra gentle. I screamed in pain. I really think that was his goal; to inflict as much pain as he could. Finally, he finished, and that is when they sent me to Forest General. I remember lying on a hospital bed where a team of about four doctors stood around discussing my condition and trying to come up with a diagnosis and treatment. I was there for about three hours, and grew very impatient with them. But again, for some reason, I was not able to talk. Finally, they decided to give up, and they sent me to some sort of specialized care hospital in Pensacola. This was my fourth hospital: Thomas, Mobile Infirmary, Forest General, and now this one. I have no idea of how I got there. In fact, the only move I remember was the bus ride to William Carey University. Select Specialized Hospital put me in the ICU, where I stayed for about three weeks or so. I was still unconscious at the time. I had a ventilator in my mouth and throat, had small white gloves on my hands, and each hand was tied to the bed frame. Let me tell you something about those little gloves. While they were on my hands, I felt even more confined, and even though my hands were tied to the bed rails, if those gloves were off, I could flex my fingers, which gave me a sense of freedom. So when the care-takers put the gloves on me, I would bow up my hands and spread my fingers to make it more difficult. I recall one nurse saying, 'You have big hands; I can hardly get these gloves on'. This made me laugh because I have small hands. I remembered my friend Sue telling me one time 'You have girl hands'. Anyway, after the attendants left, I relaxed my hands and slid them out of the gloves. Then I would put them over my freed hands so they would think they were still on my hands. Once, when I needed help and could not get their attention, I pulled off the gloves and threw them out into the room. Of course, this resulted in reattaching them and tying them much tighter. But the fact remained, I could not talk, could not move, and had no way of communicating. Occasionally, they would untie my hands and let me attempt to write a message on a white board, which turned out to be illegible most of the time. It was a terrible time. The first thing I remember in my warped mind was hearing and seeing nurses in the hallway outside my room.

Chapter Sixty-Four
Those ICU Nurses

Let's talk about these nurses. Remember, I have no idea whether this actually took place or whether it was imagined. I know I was not rational or sane, so I cannot tell you. But I could listen, and I could see, and I learned a lot about nurses. I learned that nurses are a strange breed of people. They form cliques. The ones who like each other hang together and criticize the ones whom they dislike and talk behind their backs. But this group of nurses were friends, and they talked a lot. The first thing I heard was a discussion of how much they had vested in the hospital retirement program; how much ready cash they had available; what exotic vacations they had been on, or planned to go on, to places like Mexico, Caribbean cruises, Italy, France, etc. It seemed that each one was trying to outdo and out brag the other. And they used very foul, profane, and vulgar language. I started to print the words here, but decided not to. But whatever you can imagine, they said. And to make it so sad, these were not sluts; they were not dressed in rags or like prostitutes; they were professional ladies around thirty years old. And they had small daughters and sons who were subjected to this filthy language at home. It broke my heart to hear them. Another thing they did was to ignore all calls for help from hospital patients. Ringing bells and calls for help were ignored. I recall one who went to a patient's room and yelled out at her, "Stop that," "Quit it," "Do you want me to hurt you?" I prayed I never got that nurse, but sure enough later on, I did. But in the end, I made friends with her. They also took a lot of pride in talking about their kids; from the sports they played, how smart they were, how fast they were growing up, what grade they were in, and what size shoes they wore. Again, each one tried to top the others with her own particular story.

As you can imagine, I hated every minute of my existence in the ICU. Not being able to move or speak took a toll on me, not only physically, but mentally as well, to the extent of actually going out of my mind. I had been there for twenty-one days, or at least that is what Carolyn told me. She was not allowed to see me at all during that time. So to add to my agony, I was in isolation, separated from my family and friends. Then, on a Saturday morning, Carolyn was told that she could visit me. Now this is a very sad part of the story, and it is not imagined; it actually happened just like I am telling you. I knew she was coming, but I went crazy – literally. I knew what was happening, and I knew what I was saying. I don't know how or why, but my big male nurse removed the little white glove from my right hand and untied it from the bed rail. And I recall saying, "Jesus, I had rather come live with you than to live like this, and I yanked the ventilator from my mouth. I had been told that I would die within two minutes, and I was ready to take that trip.

I wondered if I was going to get a glimpse of heaven, or have an 'out-of-body' experience, but I had neither. No revelation, but obviously, God was not ready for me yet. But can you imagine how Carolyn would have felt if she had arrived, only to be told I had committed suicide five minutes earlier? Obviously, that did not happen. What did happen was that a heavy male nurse jumped on top of me and shoved the ventilator back down my throat. I said, 'You broke my hand', and he said, 'You are not going to die on my watch'. I told him later, "I know you don't think much of God, but God used you to save my life". And I have no doubt of that at all. So, Carolyn got to come say 'Hi' to me, but I was in no shape for much of a visit. Bless her heart. I was there for at least a month, and we lived about fifty miles from the hospital, but she averaged at least five trips each week, which totaled one hundred miles round trip and took about two hours. She was truly a faithful and caring wife during that time.

I really do not know where these events took place, but I think it was during my imagined stay in Hattiesburg. I remember being told that I was going to have to return to Hattiesburg three times a week for physical therapy, and thinking 'I may as well check out houses there when I get home and move there'. But while there, I was taken to a very old and rusty outdoor amphitheater. The floor was inclined and at the end of the row of seats was a small rail car, similar to the ones they use to transmit coal from a mine, and I was forced into that little car. I recall moving very slowly up and down that rail track in that old theater. I couldn't move, but I reasoned that when it reached the end of the track, I would be able to kick the wall with my feet and free myself. The trouble was, it stopped about two feet from the wall and reversed direction, slowly beginning the uphill climb. At the bottom of the track, I saw a man standing several feet away, and I yelled at the top of my voice for help, only to be ignored. I kept expecting some sort of torture, but instead they eventually lifted me out of the car without harming me or inflicting any pain. I was pleasantly surprised to say the least.

After that, I was taken to a big white house at the top of a hill, and I suppose I was given physical therapy. One day, a lady came in and told me 'Guess what, you have been approved for an off-campus trip today. I am going to get my truck and come back for you'. This thrilled me because I had not been out of my room since arriving there. I waited for two long hours for her, and when she did finally come back, she said 'Well, I got my truck, but Paul and I are going to sit on the front porch for a few minutes before we go'. Well, another two hours passed before they returned, but finally we were loaded in the truck and took off. We were to visit a vacant house and went to the address we had been given. But the house was locked, and we didn't have a key. My escorts called the office and were told that the visit had been rescheduled for another address, but when we got there, the lady home-owner would not let us in. Some man standing in the street began telling us how mean that woman was. So much for the trip; we went back to the big house. So, I never got to see anything on my freedom ride except the inside of the cab of the truck. But I did get to go outside.

Another trip took us outside on a hiking trail through the mountains along the border of Alabama and Tennessee. It was rough going, and I was convinced that they were going to kill us along the way. So, one time when we stopped, I took my driver's license from my billfold and flung it off the cliff into the valley below. I did this to prove to whoever found it later would know that I had been there. I also placed my pistol permit on top of a flat rock for the same reason. Later, when I had regained my senses, I told Carolyn to order me a new driver's license, and she said 'Why? Your driver's license is right here in your wallet'. And I said 'That can't be; I distinctly remember throwing it off the cliff'. What about my pistol permit?' and she said 'It is here too". Now I will tell you: that really messed up my already muddled mind because I was convinced that it was real. But somehow it was not. The same thing happened all throughout these 'trips'. One day, they took me outside and laid me on the grass on a hillside and put a loud radio next to my head, but out of reach of my arms. It was blaring rap music. I don't know how long I was there. In my mind, they were as real as they could be, but if I opened my eyes, I could see I was back in my hospital room. It was like a flashback from my fantasy to reality. I never knew for sure which was which.

Okay, that is my version – four hospitals, plus the side visits. Remember, it was all very real to me. It took a long time for me to come to grips with the way it actually happened. The real version was that I was admitted to Thomas Hospital and stayed in the Intensive Care Unit for about three or four weeks, and was transferred by ambulance at 3:00 a.m. to the Specialty Hospital in Pensacola, No Mobile Infirmary; no William Carey University; no rough treatment facility; no Forest General: just the two hospitals; Thomas and Pensacola. So I had to finally let go of all those visits, although to this very day, I can describe every visit in detail. They told me that it was a result of 'Covid Fog', which is one of the side effects of the virus. There are others as well, such as those nurses I told you about. But before we get back to the hospitals, let me tell you a couple of stories.

Chapter Sixty-Five
Back to Reality

Now back to reality. All that stuff I just told you about occurred when I was in an unconscious state. What brought me back to reality was a man asking me, 'Do you live in Florida?' and I said, 'No; I live in Alabama', and he replied, 'Well, you are in Pensacola now'. I thought 'So what?' and went to sleep. That was the beginning of my conscious state in the Select Specialty Hospital. I don't know how long I had been there or what they planned to do with me. It was torture being gagged and tied down, and that is when I went crazy. I could not take it any longer, and I wanted to end it all. I was so glad to be free again.

I was told that I stayed in the ICU in that condition for about three weeks, although I had no idea of time, days, or months. I was also told that 97 people out of 100 die due to Covid when they were on a ventilator. One lady died while I was there, and another committed suicide. Finally, they moved me to a 'room' of my own. It was not a room; it was a closet, hardly big enough to accommodate a bed and a chair. But at least the ventilator was out. It was replaced by an oxygen mask. The first one they put on me was very tight and very restricted. It resembled some type of helmet, and I could not tolerate it. I remember one nurse yelling at me, "I am trying to save your life! Do you want to die?" But I yelled and yanked until they replaced it with a huge plastic mask that covered my entire face, but at least I could see and felt that I had a little bit of freedom. I got constant care in my new room. I remained in bed, flat on my back, and the attendants did everything for me.

I messed up - literally; they cleaned me up. I was hooked up to a feeding tube. In fact, from the first day, I think I spent forty-seven days on my back in bed. While at the Specialized Hospital, we met some very nice people, three of whom I want to introduce you to. I met a lady when I was in the ICU who was very nice, concerned, and made an extra effort to take care of me. She even shampooed my hair one time. Her name was Pam, and she was from Century, Florida. When I was moved to the private room, she was transferred to that hospital wing and continued to take care of me. The second person was the big male nurse I told you about earlier; the one who rammed the ventilator back down my throat after I had yanked it out. His name was Marcus, and in the beginning, I did not like him at all. I told Carolyn that he was rough and mean. In fact, I told him as well. But as time went on, and after he had saved my life, we became friends, and I came to appreciate his dedication and tenacity that he put into his job. The reality is that Carolyn won him over as a friend, and he only started being kinder to me after that. The third person was a lady named Kim. She was a Case Worker, and she was extremely helpful in making arrangements for my well-being.

I met her on occasion, but she talked to Carolyn on the phone almost daily, giving her reports on my treatment, my condition, and my progress. It was she who, along with Carolyn, got me accepted to the Colony Rehabilitation Center at Thomas. Colony was sort of like college; you had to apply for admission, and most people who applied did not get approved. Anyway, we will be forever grateful to the staff, but especially to these three.

Chapter Sixty-Six
Progress

After a couple of weeks, they helped me sit on the side of the bed and put my feet on the floor, and they exclaimed over the big progress I had made. Once they took me out into the hallway and let me stand while holding on to the banister, there again with shouts of acclamation. Then, on August 30, they decided I was well enough to go to the Colony Rehab Center at Thomas Hospital in Fairhope. This was during the time of tornado warnings from Hurricane Ida, and it was touch-and-go as to whether it was safe to travel. But to my delight, they decided to risk it. They put me in an ambulance and drove me there during the storm. Some woman sat in the back of the ambulance and yakked the entire trip. I heard about her daddy and grand-daddy and aunts and uncles and the farm she grew up on and careers and a lot more. I figured her job was to keep me from getting nervous about the transport or the weather. Anyway, after a little over an hour and we pulled up to Thomas, the very place where all this started.

Chapter Sixty-Seven
The Colony

I arrived at Colony on Monday afternoon, and I don't remember anything they did with me except to put me in a room and talk to me about what to expect while there. I had already heard that they were demanding and that they pushed their residents to their limits, so I was a bit fearful. Well, on Tuesday morning, I found out. I had four work-out sessions per day, six days a week, with only Sunday as a day of rest. I stayed there for sixteen days, and they performed a miracle. Listen, when I got there, I could not stand up. I could not get out of bed on my own. I had been flat on my back for forty-seven days, and all my leg and arm muscles had literally gone to sleep. But on that very day, they put me on the parallel bars, and with very shaky legs, I actually took six steps, and then ten. I felt like shouting. I went through a variety of exercises, too many to count, and at each step, I made significant progress. I vowed to myself that I was going to accomplish every challenge they put in front of me. I pushed as hard as I could during each exercise and exceeded their expectation. They would tell me to go a bit easier. The Therapists were conscientious and dedicated, but I learned that they were very nice, concerned, and well aware of not only my needs, but also my limitations. They encouraged me to stop and rest as often as I needed. So I got to be good friends with each of them during my sixteen-day stay.

I had one serious problem while I was there, and it centered around my prostate and bladder. I told you that I had a catheter, and at times it was pretty painful. One night, I had a blood clot that stopped up the catheter, and my bladder could not empty. Then I started experiencing what they called 'overflow spasms' every five minutes or so, where my urine flowed outside and around the tube rather than through it. The pain was almost unbearable. At three o'clock in the morning, I called for help, and a team of three women came to see what they could do. They removed the catheter, and unsuccessfully attempted to insert another one. They tried this a total of five times, each time with me groaning and moaning with an occasional scream. They kept saying that they hit my prostate and would start jabbing the catheter, trying to get past around it – or through it; I don't know. I know it did not work, and I know that they were about to kill me. Then they decided they needed to use a larger one, and I emphatically told them, "No, you are not!" I want a Urologist in here right now, and in a matter of minutes, Dr. Allen appeared. He inserted a catheter with very little pain and accessed the bladder the very first time, which gave me instant relief. So right then and there, I proclaimed him to be my Urologist and told Carolyn to cancel the appointment I had with another doctor. This also happened one Saturday night at our house, and I spent five hours in the South Baldwin Hospital in the Foley emergency room on Sunday.

One week later, I had an appointment with Dr. Allen, and he performed surgery on my prostate and corrected the problem. Now I am functioning normally and enjoying life again. I went from a wheelchair, to a scooter, and a walker, and a cane, and am now pretty much self-sufficient, much to Carolyn's delight. I am still weak, and sometimes dizzy, but am told that is normal. I started physical therapy at Encore the following week, and regained my strength quite rapidly.

Oh, after all this was over, my wife persuaded me to get the two Covid shots and the Booster. So I thought it was all over for me. Wrong!

Chapter Sixty-Eight
Covid-19 Twice More

I caught Covid again about a year and a half later. This time, it was not bad; just sort of like a bad cold or sinus infection, and it passed after a few days. I did not go to the doctor.

Then, on October 4, 2024, my sister picked me up and drove me to Thomas Hospital, where Carolyn was a patient. We were there to get her discharged so we could transport her to a Recovery Center. However, I was not well or steady. When I walked through the Emergency Room door, I stumbled and had to catch the wall to keep from falling. The nurse sitting at the admissions desk saw me and told me to come over there. I explained I was there to pick up my wife, but she told me I could do that after they examined me. I never made it upstairs to get my wife. My sister had to do that without me. I was immediately admitted to the hospital with COVID-19, and I was there for five days. So I never saw my wife go to the Recovery Center. And the day I got discharged and went to see her was the day she was being transported by ambulance to the University Hospital, where she died one day later.

Chapter Sixty-Nine
Prayer Works

I want to tell you this: I don't have any idea of how many people were praying for me during my major bout with Covid. I know there were a half-dozen churches or more, plus friends, neighbors, family, and even people who I did not know and who did not know me. One such lady later told me, 'I saw your name on a prayer list, and I remembered 'Duck, " so I prayed for you regularly. But I am convinced that God is the one who brought me through it. I overheard the doctors saying on two occasions, 'We're losing him' and 'He's turning blue'. That is when the doctors told Carolyn to prepare for my funeral; that I was not going to survive. I was also told that very few people who have been on a ventilator for as long as I was ever survived; only three of one hundred. So, all the praise and glory and thanks go to God alone. Without Him, I would not be here today typing this account.

Chapter Seventy
Missed Opportunities

Now that I am old, looking back on my life, I realized that I have missed several major opportunities along the way. I should have studied more in high school, even though I did okay. One significant opportunity I failed to pursue was a job offer at Brookley Air Force Base in Mobile. When I was a Senior in High School, I took a Civil Service Exam and scored a high grade. This got me an interview with the Brookley official, and I was later offered a job in their Electronics Division. I would have gone to electronic school for four hours each morning and would have worked in the lab for another four hours each afternoon. It was a four-year course, and at the end of the four years, I would have had a degree in Electronic Engineering and would have held the grade of GS-11. The only thing I lacked to begin work was an ID badge, and I went to Brookley to have it issued to me. But instead, I followed Dad's advice and told them I had decided to go to college in September, and it would not be fair to them for me to take the job and quit three months later. What a mistake this may have been. I could have retired from the Government at age 58 with forty years of service. I have often wondered how my life would have turned out if I had taken this job. As it turned out, I retired with the rank of GS-14 after only twenty-five years at the age of 64. But I cannot cry over spilled milk, and I am not disappointed at the career I have had.

I should have taken college more seriously and selected some more difficult subjects than I did. I should have explored the business world more carefully and decided which field of study was my passion. Instead, I took jobs that were offered and never really settled down in one area of business.

And certainly I should have kept my nose cleaned much better than I did. I have been easily influenced by some people who have led me down a path of moral ineptitude and adultery, decisions that still haunt me to this day. I should have paid much more attention to the instructions and the warnings written in the book of Proverbs.

Chapter Seventy-One
So What's Next

Well, I guess this is about all that I wanted to say. And I guess the obvious question is 'Why did I write all this anyway?' I am not really sure. As I said at the beginning, I wanted a simple book about a simple man that the average man and woman could understand. And maybe they can identify with some of the stuff that is in this book. It is my hope that maybe someone can find a little hope and encouragement by reading my story. Maybe someone who is facing a crisis or going through a calamity of their own can find comfort with someone who can sympathize and empathize with them. Maybe someone can see the mistakes I have made in my life and use my experiences to avoid making those mistakes in their own life or pulling themselves out of a bad situation. It may be that someone is living a life right now that they know is wrong, but they feel trapped. Please know that if you want to change your path, it is possible to do so. The Good Lord knows I have made dozens of wrong choices and some pretty stupid decisions. You know, all through the book of Proverbs, Solomon reminds us to think before we act and to seek the counsel of the wise people around us. Man, I sure could have avoided a lot of turmoil and pain if I had followed that advice. So if you have read this far, first of all, Thank You for sticking it out, and secondly, please think before you speak; think before you leap; and above all, pray about everything.

So what's next for me? I don't know. We all live life one day at a time, don't we? We all do that, whether we want to or not. We don't know the toll that Covid-19 will take or how many will succumb to its infection. I may kick the bucket before another year passes. I am eighty-two now; my mother died at age seventy-eight. However, my Dad lived until he was ninety-eight. I do know this. My time here on this earth and my journey until my time is over are in the hands of the Almighty God. And that is good enough for me. May God bless you real good. Good-bye.

Chapter Seventy-Two
The Little New House
2025

Remember back when we were house hunting, we saw another one that we liked. We were just riding around one Sunday afternoon and happened upon a subdivision called Greenbriar in Foley. We went to the model home, met the representative, and told him what we liked. He showed us a floorplan and took us to a home under construction with that plan. We went home and talked it over. Carolyn reminded me that everything we were connected to was in Spanish Fort – church, doctors, drug stores, friends, grocery, veterinarians – everything we dealt with on a regular basis. She said, 'If we move to Foley, thirty-two miles away, we will be making trips back to Spanish Fort every two or three days. I said, 'You are right. We called the representative and told him we had decided not to move. After Carolyn died, I sold her Mercedes and had a huge yard sale where I sold our Christmas decorations, her clothes, her shoes, and some of our appliances and furniture. Then I called the representative we had talked to months earlier and told him I was interested in his house. I sold our house in February 2025 and bought his house that same day. And that is the house I am living in today. What an ending to a long story.